COVER PHOTOS

EARLY NEWFOUNDLAND SETTLEMENT

TOP: **A FANCIFUL DEPICTION OF JOHN GUY'S 1612 ENCOUNTER WITH THE BEOTHUKS IN TRINITY BAY.** From Theodor de Bry, *America (Historia Americæ sive Novi Orbis)*, pt. XIII, German, edited by Matthaeus Merian (Frankfurt: Caspar Rôtel, 1628, 1634) 7. Copy courtesy of the CIHM/ICMH (Canadian Institute for Historical Microreproductions) microfiche series; no. 94749 in the Queen Elizabeth II Library at Memorial University of Newfoundland, St. John's, Newfoundland. Original housed in The National Library of Canada, Ottawa, Ontario.

BOTTOM: **MAP OF FERRYLAND, 1693.** From D.W. Prowse, *A History of Newfoundland from the English, Colonial, and Foreign Records*, 2nd edition (London: Eyre and Spottiswoode, 1896) 111. Caption beneath image reads, "Ferryland, showing Baltimore's House. From Fitzburgh's map, 1693." Image modified by Duleepa Wijayawardhana, 1999.

FERRYLAND

Library and Archives Canada Cataloguing in Publication

Fardy, Bernard D., 1949-
   Ferryland : the colony of Avalonia / B.D. Fardy.

ISBN 1-894463-78-1

   1. Ferryland (N.L.)--History. 2. Baltimore, George
Calvert, Baron, 1580?-1632. 3. Great Britain--Colonies--America.
I. Title.

FC2199.F47F37 2005   971.8   C2005-904209-5

PRINTED IN CANADA

FLANKER PRESS
ST. JOHN'S, NL, CANADA
TOLL FREE: 1-866-739-4420
WWW.FLANKERPRESS.COM

We acknowledge the financial support of: the Government of Canada through the Book
Publishing Industry Development Program (BPIDP); the Canada Council for the Arts which
last year invested $20.3 million in writing and publishing throughout Canada; the
Government of Newfoundland and Labrador, Department of Tourism, Culture and
Recreation.

FERRYLAND

THE COLONY OF AVALONIA

B. D. Fardy

FLANKER PRESS LTD.
ST. JOHN'S, NL
2005

For Larry
who loved a good comic book.

Acknowledgements

The author wishes to express thanks to the following individuals, organizations and institutions for their generous help and cooperation in the writing of this brief history of the Colony of "Avalonia."

Special thanks to Keith Mooney and Annette Mooney for generous contributions of photos and other illustrative material, and leads to sources of material about their historic community, as well as their many "express messenger" trips. Particular thanks to Mrs. Dorothy Agriesti, unofficial historian of the town, for reading the manuscript and making corrections, and offering valuable comments and suggestions. Also for her generous access to her personal collection of information about many of the unknown persons and incidents of the town and its 400 year history. Much gratitude to the Town of Ferryland, the Ferryland Development Association, and the Southern Shore Folk Arts Council for their cooperation and contributions of illustrative material and other information.

Thanks also to Mrs. Lil Hawkins of the Colony of Avalon Foundation for her assistance and access to the Foundation's collections, laboratory and other facilities and to the personnel of the Ferryland Museum and all others from the "Capital" of the "Shore" who have over the years reminded me of my own Irish roots with their lively and hospitable fashions. And may "None of Us Fear the Wind as Long as Our Haystacks are Tied Down!"

Thanks also to a Friend Indeed.

Appreciation is also expressed for copies of and permission to use illustrative and other document materials from the collections of: Memorial University of Newfoundland — Centre for Newfoundland Studies; the Provincial Archives of Newfoundland and Labrador; The Newfoundland Museum; the Newfoundland Military Museum; Parks Canada; the A. C. Hunter Library — Newfoundland Centre; the Newfoundland and Labrador Heritage WS (MUN); Mrs. Michelle O'Connell and The Colony Cafe, Ferryland; and the Town of Ferryland. Special thanks to Cindy of the Blinkin' Light Computer Co.

Table of Contents

Author's Note

The "Colony of Avalon" as it is being called today, was in its earliest years known by chroniclers and cartographers by its original designation by Sir George Calvert, Lord Baltimore, as Avalonia. This designation of the name is used throughout the text in keeping with the "olde" English name. It first appears on the map of John Mason of 1629, very soon after Mason visited Newfoundland and had spent about six years on the island surveying and mapping it. Baltimore's colony on the Avalon Peninsula as being called Avalonia is shown in the block on the map below.

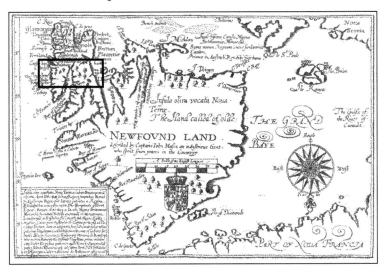

John Mason's map — 1629.

A later map made by Captain Robert Robinson, Royal Navy, in 1669, "An exact Mapp of Newfounde Land so far as the English and French Fishing trade is concerned," shows that the Avalon Peninsula area of the Island of Newfoundland was still being referred to as the "Province Avalonia" almost fifty years after Baltimore had established it. In more recent times the name has been modernized into the present form of Avalon from the "olde" English appellation of Avalonia.

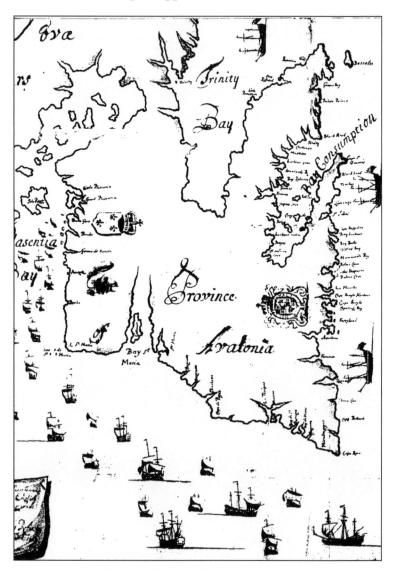

French trading to and from Placentia Bay.

Sir George Calvert, Lord Baltimore. (Photo: Enoch Pratt Free Library: Baltimore, Maryland.)

The Calvert Coat of Arms. This Coat of Arms was significantly altered from the original by Lord Baltimore's son Cecil after he had established the Colony of Maryland in 1633, to incorporate elements of his mother's family Arms, the Croslands. The pair of leopard supporters were also removed and replaced with the figures of a fisherman and a "planter," or farmer. (Photo: Horwood and De Viser: *Historic Newfoundland*, 1986. [MUN-CNS].)

INTRODUCTION

FERRYLAND is believed to have first been named by the Portuguese *Farelhao*, meaning "steep little island" or "reef" or "headland," all of which could apply when the chain of islands and the "Downs" are considered at the approach to Ferryland harbour. Once the French began to use the harbour, the name became *Forillon*, meaning "cape" or "point." It was finally corrupted into the English "Ferryland" after being translated into some fanciful versions such as Freizeland, Fair-Ellen, and Ferriland. The name Ferryland was in common usage even in Lord Baltimore's time and was officially recognized by the Newfoundland government in the 1830s during the colony's fight to gain Responsible Government.

Its proximity to the bountiful fish stocks of the Grand Banks made it a desirable location for all the countries who competed in the trade. For a time in the mid 1500s it rivalled St. John's and Harbour Grace as the most important "fishing station" of the colony. With the influx of settlers in the early 1800s its small harbour was found not to be nearly large enough to accommodate large-scale commercial operations.

Ferryland became Newfoundland's third commercial settlement in 1620 under the tutelage of Sir George Calvert, Lord Baltimore. In its more than 400 year history it suffered successive wars that saw the settlement repeatedly destroyed or ravaged, but the Colony of Avalonia survives today with a stable economy and a rich and historic heritage that holds one of Newfoundland's most unique treasures.

opiniones personnae...
...facta omnibus.

opinions belong to persons...
...facts belong to everybody.

CHAPTER I

The Machinations of Colonization

The Colony of Avalonia which today has become synony-
mous with the community of Ferryland on the
Southern Shore of the Avalon Peninsula of Newfoundland,
has a long, colourful, and convoluted history dating back to
1497 when the "new-founde-lande" was officially discovered
by John Cabot. Political intrigues, Royal patronage, and
mercantile machinations all played their parts in shaping the
development and destiny of the "new world." Ferryland and
the Colony of Avalonia was to be a catalyst in that development, not only in Newfoundland, but on the continent of
North America as well.

More than 100 years before Sir George Calvert, later Lord
Baltimore, established his Colony of Avalonia, Bristol
merchants had been trading from the New-founde-lande.
They had competition. The French, Portuguese, Spanish and
Dutch were all interested in exploring and exploiting the fish-
rich waters off Newfoundland's coasts.

The Bristol merchants had already sponsored a half-dozen
voyages to the west, and only partially to find a northwest
passage to the spice-rich lands of the Orient. They had been
trading with the Icelanders for their "stock fish," dried and
salted north Atlantic cod, and were paying dearly for it. The

Icelanders knew the route to the Grand Banks off Newfoundland as their ancestors, the Vikings, had already discovered Newfoundland 500 years before Cabot.

The Bristol traders wanted to know the location of, and route to the cod fish grounds so they could send their own ships there and thus eliminate the middlemen of the trade — the Icelanders. From their trading missions to Iceland and the Scandinavian countries they learned of the Viking voyages to "Vinland" and of their northern route to the New World.

By 1496 they had convinced King Henry VII of England that they could find a route to the far east by way of a north-west passage, rather than by the elusive southwest one sought by Columbus and the Spaniards. King Henry sanctioned the voyage since it did not interfere with the ventures of the Spanish in the Caribbean or the Portuguese who were looking for a southeast passage through Africa.

By the early 1500s the Spanish had already laid claim to everything in the western hemisphere, including Newfoundland. The Portuguese also laid claim to the island by virtue of the voyages of the *Corte Reals*, and the French after the voyages of *Cartier* in the 1530s. The French were to prove to be the real contenders.

In the 1530s, the political and religious maps of Europe had changed drastically. The squabbling Spanish and Portuguese kingdoms had been declared a dual kingdom by the Pope in Rome and their claims in the New World divided by a *linea divisionis*, an arbitrary line of longitude in the mid-Atlantic which saw everything west of the line belong to Spain and everything east of it to Portugal. The New-founde-lande of the north was not included in the papal bull so the French considered they had just as much right to claim it as their Catholic cousins in England. By the turn of the 17th century the French had established themselves on the North American continent in a "New France" and considered the south, west, and northeast coasts of the island of Newfoundland to be their territory.

The French didn't recognize the English claim to sovereignty over the island as proclaimed by Sir Humphrey Gilbert in 1583. They were satisfied to allow the English to fish from Cape Race to Cape Bonavista on the east coast, but in no other areas. In 1608 the French announced that they had established a New France on the continent of North America at *Quebec*, far up the St. Lawrence River in the heart of the mainland near the island of New-founde-lande.

France had recently become the dominant power in Europe following the failure of the Spanish to invade England in 1588 and the destruction of its great Armada by the Royal Navy and savage storms. The English now feared that the French colonization of continental America would lead to their claiming their cod-rich "island of fish" — the New-found-land.

To counter the French threat, the English merchants prevailed on the king to relent on the more than 100-year-old policy of not allowing any settlement on the island. In 1610, King James I granted the London and Bristol Company of merchants a Charter to "inhabite and establishe a Colony or Colonies in the Southerne and Easterne p'tes of the country and islande commonlie called Newfoundland..."

The first attempt was made by one of the Company's native sons of Bristol, John Guy, who came out to Newfoundland with forty prospective colonizers that same year and settled at a site in Conception Bay they named Cupids. After three years of harsh winters, pirate raids, and an unyielding land, Guy quit his attempt and returned to England.

The London and Bristol Company then looked for others to continue their efforts. In 1617 Sir William Vaughan, a Welsh gentleman, romantic, and writer of some renown, received a grant to a tract of land on the southern end of the Avalon Peninsula. Vaughan had dreams of establishing a New Wales in America and sent out a party of Welsh colonizers to begin a plantation at what would become the community of Renews. But it seems the Welsh proved to be not very good colonizers, and within two years Vaughan had abandoned his attempt at establishing a plantation in Newfoundland. With his failure, Vaughan was compelled to sell off much of his huge land grant. One buyer was Sir George Calvert, later to become Lord Baltimore.

Sir George Calvert. He founded the Colony of Avalonia and the settlement of Ferryland in 1621 but soon quit it and moved to "Mary's Land" in the New England colonies around 1632. (Photo: Memorial University Newfoundland, Centre for Newfoundland Studies [Hereinafter MUN-CNS].)

Calvert was born at Kipling in Yorkshire, England probably in 1580 (some sources say 1578/79), the son of a well-to-do family. His father Leonard, thought to have been Flemish, married into an old Yorkshire family, the Croslands (or Crosslands) whose history dated back in that area to 1366.

Calvert was well-educated, entering Trinity College at Oxford around the age of fourteen in 1594. A Latin scholar, he acquired a Bachelor's degree in three years and an honourary Master of Arts degree by 1604. On November 22 of that year he married Anne Mynne, daughter of a prominent family of Hertfordshire, at St. Peter's, Cornhill, London. During the next eighteen years the Calverts had eleven children, six sons and five daughters.

He travelled Europe extensively in his early years and learned several languages, including French, Spanish and

Italian. By 1606 he had come to the attention of Sir Robert Cecil, England's Secretary of State and King James I's chief advisor and policy maker. Cecil prevailed on Calvert to become his personal secretary and Calvert continued in that position until Cecil's death in 1612. In Cecil's employ he advanced in the Civil Service increasing his position and influence and soon became a trusted confidant of the King himself.

During these years Calvert held several positions of importance and influence and was also elected a member of Parliament for Bossiny in Cornwall. He did special envoy missions for the king to both France and Spain and was appointed clerk of the Privy Council which gave him the ear of the king. He also served on three commissions of inquiry into the state of affairs in Ireland, which at the time was in religious upheaval.

In 1617 he was knighted and two years later elevated to the position of Secretary of State. In this capacity he defended the king in Parliament in his unpopular efforts to forge an alliance with either of the Catholic nations of France or Spain. France was steadily growing in power since the decline of Spain after the defeat of its Armada, and James was concerned about his claims in the New World and France's competition with him there. He was looking for an ally and believed Spain, since they also had interests there that could be threatened by the French, would be a likely partner. Young Calvert agreed with him believing the Spanish could be the "better friend or more formidable foe."

It became Calvert's task then for the next several years to try to forge this alliance by arranging a royal marriage between James's son Prince Charles and the Spanish Princess *Infanta* Maria, daughter of King Philip III. The English Parliament opposed the alliance but Calvert supported the king both as his advisor and as a member of Parliament. For his loyalty Calvert won great rewards.

In 1621 the king granted him a manor estate in Longford County, Ireland with land holdings of some 2,300 acres. By now Calvert was becoming a wealthy man, partly due to the king having granted him special favour in the silk trade, and he built his own family estate which he called Kilpin Hall at Boulton-on-Swale in Yorkshire very near his childhood home. At the same time James also granted him title to that part of the Avalon Peninsula in Newfoundland where he would attempt to establish his Colony of Avalonia.

Kilpin Hall: The Calvert Estate in Yorkshire, England, was built by Calvert and passed down through his family for generations. (Photo: The Enoch Pratt Free Library, Baltimore, Maryland.)

He acquired a large tract of the area of the Avalon Peninsula that had been sold to Vaughan by the London and Bristol Company after Guy had abandoned his attempt at colonization there in 1613. Calvert's grant included all the land of the Avalon Peninsula south of "the Plantacion [sic] of St. John's and John Guy's colony of Bristol's Hope (Cupids), south to Ferryland Harbour and west to Placentia Bay." Vaughan was reluctant to sell off all his grant as he still believed he could establish a New Wales in the New World. King James would not part with the colony of St. John's which had been established by Gilbert's claim.

It has long been debated why Calvert undertook his venture of colonization. Some suggest it was purely a mercenary adventure, and given his investments in the Virginia and East India Companies it probably was. Others believe he was a philanthropist, humanitarian, and religious zealot who truly believed he could establish a safe haven for persecuted and impoverished Irish Catholics from Ireland, and those already economically and spiritually deprived on the island of Newfoundland.

There is no doubt that Calvert was a successful businessman. After his death, his son Cecil who later ran the colony of Maryland, said that his father had expended some twenty to thirty thousand pounds on his venture in Avalonia. In today's money values that amount could come to well over four million dollars. One can only wonder where he could come up with such money given his modest employment as a simple civil servant.

Calvert had money. In 1609 he had invested a thousand pounds in the newly formed East India Company. By 1616 he had also invested a substantial amount in the Virginia Company in America which was hoping to establish a "New England" on the continent in response to the French declaration that they had established a New France there.

After his purchase from the Vaughan grant in Newfoundland, Calvert bought into the New England Company in 1622 and with his exemptions granted him by the king in the silk trade had been making himself a very tidy income. So it would appear that in 1620 when he bought his plantation in Newfoundland his interests were clearly mercantile ones. Yet they appear not to have been his only ones.

Calvert's piously chosen name for his colony gives some insight into the dichotomy of his motives and perhaps his philosophy. As well as being wealthy, educated, travelled, and business minded, he seemed also to be a deeply religious man.

He was, at least overtly, of the Anglican faith, as were most people in England at this time, since it was barely a hundred years since Henry VIII's Reformation and the adoption of Protestantism. The Thirty Years War had just begun in Europe and was spilling over into the British Isles by 1620. The War was a religious one basically and Calvert may have been on a surreptitious but perilous path to establish a safe haven for Catholics who were outwardly beginning to be persecuted in England.

Baltimore also appears to have been somewhat of a romantic. He was a devoted follower of the Arthurian legend — Camelot, King Arthur, and the Knights of the Round Table. By the end of the first millennium, the death of King Arthur, the disappearance of Camelot, and the Knights of the Round Table had interwoven pagan Celtic myth with Christian Celtic legend.

In pagan Celtic mythology Avalon was the afterworld where the dead were transformed into another, higher existence, much the same as the Christian belief in Heaven. It was the domain of *Avallach, Lord of the Dead*, and eventually evolved into Celtic myth to be an island called Avalon, believed to lie somewhere to the west.

By the end of the 1100s, Christianity had been well established in the British Isles, but many of the people there had been merely coated with a thin veneer of it. Somerset's Isle of Glass became the site of an early Christian Abbey later to be called Glastonbury. According to legend, it was here that Joseph of Aramathea, who had given up his own burial vault to Christ, journeyed to in his very late life with the Holy Grail.

Glastonbury for the fledgling Christians of Britain was the aged Celtic equivalent of Avalon. Here the pagan Celtic and Christian Celtic melded. It was to the Island of Avalon that King Arthur was ferried to recover from his wounds to someday return, to once again rule Britain from a new Camelot.

The religious parallels are at once apparent and at first glance Calvert would seem to be either an incurable romantic or a religious zealot. Perhaps he fancied himself a modern day Joseph of Arimethea, who would establish the first Christian Church in the heathen lands of America. The truth probably lies somewhere in between — he was first and foremost a pragmatist. He undertook his ventures into colonization to make money, and possibly attain position and perhaps even power or fame. Yet some of that pragmatism also included a genuine desire to see religious tolerance practiced by all sects of the Christian religion — Protestants and Catholics alike.

The name Calvert chose for his colony in Newfoundland — Avalonia — was Anglicized from the scholastic Latin to the modern English Avalon and it came eventually to designate the entire eastern peninsula of the island as it is known today. Calvert's true motives for his aspirations to colonization can only be speculated upon. He already had substantial land holdings in England and Ireland and financial interests in foreign trading companies. He was also well acquainted with Lord Falkland, Sir Henry Carey, who was Viscount of Ireland and who had also recently attained two large grants of land in Newfoundland, one of them directly bordering Calvert's grant on the southern Avalon Peninsula.

What may have begun for Calvert as a purely business venture may have become a crusade in humanitarianism and philanthropy to see religious equality in a time when the Church was in turmoil all across Europe. Since the advent of Protestantism against the Church of Rome, schisms among the Protestant movement were rampant.

Like Vaughan before him, Calvert was for several years an absentee landlord. His "affairs of state" trying to arrange the royal marriage between England and Spain occupied all his time as he shuttled between the two countries on His Majesty's service. Again, like Vaughan, he hired a governor to establish and administer his colony. In the spring of 1621 he sent one Captain Wynn (variously spelled Wynne or Winne) and twelve Welshmen to start up his Colony of Avalonia.

Captain Wynn and his colony builders arrived in Ferryland Harbour on August 4, 1621. But they found the place was not deserted. By now the harbour had been a favoured seasonal fishing station for men of Spain, Portugal, France and now England for almost 100 years. Just the previous summer a Dutch trader, one Captain de Vries, on a venture to buy salt cod from fishermen in Newfoundland found the harbour quite occupied. He reported that he entered "a place called 'Ferrelandt.' There [he] found seven or eight fishermen. [He] wanted to buy their fish, but everyone of them had already sold his catch." However, Wynn reported no difficulties with anyone he may have found there and perhaps they were willing to accept and cooperate with the new ownership.

Calvert's governor immediately set to work establishing his master's Colony of Avalonia. Wynn and his colonists, all men, were sent as builders and as such were all skilled craftsmen and artisans. Carpenters, stone-cutters, masons and a salt maker were among his crew, and their employer must have offered them substantial incentives for they went about their work quite seriously. They were all Welshmen, just as Vaughan's had been in 1617, but his crew had proved to be not very industrious and their failure had led to his selling some of his grant to Calvert.

Wynn's Welshmen, however, proved to be very industrious indeed. As it appeared to turn out a few years later, they were more assiduous for themselves than they were for their patron. Between their arrival in August and the end of October they did an admirable job of completing their habitation. They had built a stone house intended to be the governor's residence: 44 feet by 15 feet, consisting of a hall, a cellar, and four other chambers. By Christmas Wynn and his crew had completed a kitchen with a chimney and another chamber over it consisting of four rooms — in all likelihood bedrooms which would be dry and warm in the wet and cold winter to come.

BALTIMORE'S GRANT   1623

BALTIMORE'S
Letters "Patent" - Grant
By Royal Charter of James 1
1623

"THE CHARTER OF AVALON

JAMES By The Grace Of God, King; *Whereas our right trusty Counsellor Sir George Calvert being excited with a laudable and pious zeale to enlarge the extent of the Christian world and therewith of our Empire hath heretofore to his coste purchased a certain region in the country of ours called Newfoundland not yet husbanded or planted though in certain parts thereof inhabited by certain barbarous peoples: And intending now to transport thither a very great colony of the English Nation hath humbly besought us to confirm all the said region with certain priveledges requisite for good government.*

POWERS

Civil Rights to as full as the Bishop of Durham. Region to be held in capito by Knight's service, yeilding a fifth part of all gold and silver. That the region may be Eminent above all other parts of Newfoundland and graced with larger titles we have thought fitt to erect the same into a Province, to be called the Province of Avalon. Power to make laws, appoint judges; to Pardon, in an emergency to make special laws without the consent of the freeholder; to muster and train men and to declare Martial Law; to confer title and incorporate towns. To be free from all customs and power to import and export to England and all foreign countries all goods for ten years; after which to pay such customs as our subjects are bound to pay and no more. Power to constitute ports of entry, at which all ships must unlade and lade, any custom to the contrary not withstanding..... Power to enjoy all customs payable or accruing.

Signed at Westminster *(James I)*
The 7 of April
In the 21 Year of Our Reign of England.

Baltimore's Grant.

In the spring of 1622, Wynn reported to Calvert the "...good tydings of all our healths, safety and good success in our proceedings." He said that he and his men had spent the winter, which apparently must have been a very mild one, breaking ground to sow spring crops of wheat, barley, oats, and vegetables, and building a palisade of seven-foot-high wooden stakes lashed together with ropes and nails as a protection against pirate raids.

He also dug a sixteen-foot-deep well near the governor's house, even though he reported that the freshwater streams quenched their thirst as "well as any beere...and never offended our stomachs at all..." While they waited for their crops to appear, the men built a second lodging house, a brew house, and a hen house. They completed their forge and had their salt works in operation by early summer.

By late 1622 Wynn had further enclosed his settlement in "palizado [palisade] onto the Plantation about foure acres of ground, for the keeping off of both man and beast, with post and rayle seven foot high, sharpened in the toppe, the trees being pitched upright and fastened with spikes and nayles."

Wynn also gave a favourable report of their agricultural endeavours, which was considered a must if the colony was to survive. He reported that: "...we have Wheat, Oates, Barley, Pease, and Beanes about the quantity of two acres. Of Garden roome about half an acre; the corne though late sowne is now in earing; the Beanes and the goodliest Pease that I ever saw, have flourished in their blooms this twenty dayes. We have a plentiful kitchin garden of Lettuce, Raddish, Carrets, Coleworts, Turneps, and many other things. We have also at this present [time] a flourishing medow of at least three Acres, with many hay-cocks of exceeding good hay and hope to fit a great deale more against another yeare."

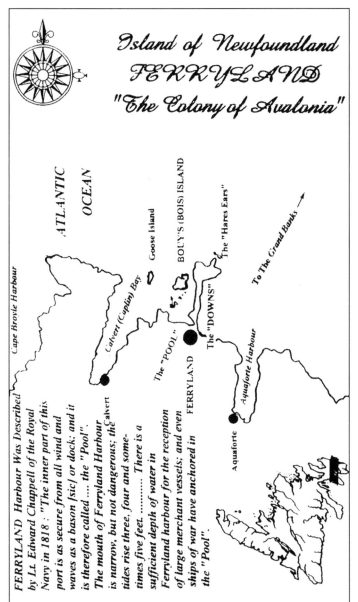

Island of Newfoundland
FERRYLAND
"The Colony of Avalonia"

ATLANTIC

OCEAN

Cape Brovle Harbour

Calvert (Caplin) Bay

Goose Island

BOU'S (BOIS) ISLAND

The "Hares Ears"

The "POOL"

The "DOWNS"

FERRYLAND

Calvert

Aquaforte Harbour

To The Grand Banks

Aquaforte

FERRYLAND Harbour Was Described by Lt. Edward Chappell of the Royal Navy in 1818: "The inner part of this port is as secure from all wind and waves as a bason [sic] or dock; and it is therefore called .... the "Pool". The mouth of Ferryland Harbour is narrow, but not dangerous; the tides rise three, four and sometimes five feet. .... There is a sufficient depth of water in Ferryland harbour for the reception of large merchant vessels; and even ships of war have anchored in the "Pool".

Map — Ferryland: "The Colony of Avalonia." (Map: B.F.)

15

Later that year, Wynn sent a second report of his progress to Calvert in which he asked for more supplies as well as more people. He requested that: "humbly praying, your Honour, that I may be furnished with all necessary tools and provision of victuals the next year; and if your Honour may, with about the number of twenty persons more.... Women would be necessary here for many respects." It seemed now that Wynn had his habitation built he now wanted to populate it.

Wynn's glowing account of his progress and production in his first year and a half would have been suspect to anyone who was even vaguely familiar with the terrain and climate of Newfoundland. But Calvert had never been across the big pond and received his governor's reports with great satisfaction and enthusiasm. He was so pleased and encouraged that he granted Wynn's every request and the next year he enlisted a second company of colonizers to head out to his Avalonia.

PROFILE — The British Colonies

The Newfoundland colonies of the 1600s, most accept, began with John Guy's settlement at Cupids in 1610. Some suggest that they began with Sir Humphrey Gilbert's claim to the island under the rule of Elizabeth I in 1583. From 1610 to 1620 when King James I embarked on his period of colonization of Newfoundland, none of the patents or grants issued were allowed to infringe on what was already considered to be the Colony of St. John's. This colony, considered to have been established by Gilbert took in all the land from Cape St. Francis on the northern tip of the eastern peninsula of the Avalon, south to Cape Spear and west to Holyrood on the east coast of Conception Bay.

When the wealthy and powerful London and Bristol Company approached King James I, he gave them a patent to the remainder of the Avalon Peninsula, but would not relent on the already granted territory of the Colony of St. John's, which he considered already established by Gilbert.

The Bristol merchant princes chose a native son, John Guy, to set up their colony on the Avalon. Guy set sail in the spring of 1610 with forty prospective colonists and chose a site in Conception Bay, which he called Cupids. His group experienced a mild winter and by the following spring had completed their houses and stores.

The next year was not so easy. Guy had trouble with the West Country Merchants Company, a rival of the London and Bristol Company, who wanted the island to remain a seasonal fishing station. Their agents, the ruthless and often brutal fishing admirals, harassed Guy's planters, as the settlers were commonly called, and the following year he was raided by pirates who burned the tiny settlement to the ground and carried off many of the inhabitants.

Sir Humphrey Gilbert took possession of the "New-founde-lande" in 1583 for Queen Elizabeth I of England by simply landing in St. John's harbour and planting her flag and Royal Coat of Arms, thus establishing the first British colony in North America. (Photos: B.F. Newfoundland Museum [Hereinafter NM].)

The third winter was a severe one weather wise, and many of the remaining settlers grew ill with the scurvy, eight of them dying. Guy gave up his effort, despairing that it could ever succeed in the lawlessness and harsh climate of the island. He returned to Bristol in 1613 where he soon became Mayor of the town and eventually a respected magistrate.

The London and Bristol Company then looked for others to continue their venture. In 1617, Sir William Vaughan, a Welsh gentleman of some means and vision, acquired a large tract of the southern portion of the Avalon Peninsula. Vaughan had visions of creating a New Wales, or Cambriol

Colchos as he called it, in America just as the French were trying to establish a New France. He sent out a party of colonizers to establish a settlement at what would later become the community of Renews on the Southern Shore of the peninsula.

But the Welsh would turn out to be poor pioneers. Vaughan, like many of the grantees to come after him, was an absentee landlord who never visited his holdings, leaving the development and administration of his colony to his governor. One of them was an accomplished Navy officer, Richard Whitbourne, lately Knighted. Sir Richard crossed the Atlantic in 1618 to check on the progress of Vaughan's colony and reported that the colonists had not even built themselves proper houses for the winter weather. A year later he reported that the "Welch fooles" had abandoned the colony and left the island altogether.

The next year Vaughan sent out another contingent of colonists who located themselves farther south at Trepassey, perhaps in the hope that a more southerly locale would prove to have a milder climate. This effort also ended in failure commercially because of pirate raids.

Vaughan, as an absentee landlord, had other overseas investments, held a position as a Justice of the Peace, and was engaged in his writing to promote the settlement of the New World, particularly Newfoundland. He wrote several treatises on his proposals for settlement and commerce, notably his *Newlander's Cure*, and his extensive book *The Golden Fleece* in which he extolled the prospects of Newfoundland even though he had never been there.

He had the ear of King James at his court however, and pressed his ideas to cultivate trade from Newfoundland. He was also losing money. The London and Bristol Company who had sold him the charter to the Newfoundland real estate was also having trouble with the New England

Company which was developing a colony in Virginia. Vaughan, siding with his benefactors, argued in King James's court that cod fish caught on the Grand Banks of Newfoundland could be shipped to England cheaper and quicker than fish from the New England colonies simply because Newfoundland was closer.

The competition between the two companies was sharp: indeed one of the "erring captaines" who had raided Vaughan's ships sent out to reinforce and supply his colony at Trepassey in 1618 "went forth with Sir Walter Raleigh...," one of Queen Elizabeth's champions who was by now a major shareholder in the New England and Virginia Companies.

King James fancied himself as a bit of a visionary, romantic, and literary scholar also. He indulged Vaughan's ideas and when his colony began to fail three years after he began it, the king allowed Vaughan to sell off portions of it despite the protests of the London and Bristol Company. The New England and Virginia Companies were under the control of such Knights as Raleigh and David Kirke, favourites of his detested predecessor Elizabeth I, the virgin queen whom he more properly thought of as the "barren bitch" Queen who had cut off the head of his mother, Mary Queen of Scots, who had proved to be so quite contrary.

In 1620 Vaughan sold off a large portion of his grant to Sir George Calvert. It included all the land south of Guy's grant to the area just north of Renews where he was trying to establish his own colony. Vaughan and Calvert were old friends and had been fellow students at Oxford, and as another contemporary put it, "in a natural way, as one pawns off a worthless horse on a friend, so Sir William sold a large portion of his grant at a very high price to Lord Baltimore."

When Calvert sent out his first contingent of colonizers in 1621 they were Welshmen and it may have been a condition of the sale that his settlers be Welsh. In his book promoting settlement in Newfoundland, Vaughan lamented: "I am sorry to find so many hopeless in my country of Wales whereas close by us in Devonshire 150 ships go to Newfoundland transporting from thence those commodities without which Spain and Italy can hardly live...." The "commodities" he referred to was salt codfish.

At the same time as his sale to Calvert, Vaughan sold another portion of his grant to Sir Henry Carey, Lord Falkland of Ireland who was also Lord Deputy of that country. Carey and Calvert were old friends also and their years in Ireland together had made them kindred spirits. Together they dreamed of creating a New Ireland just as their benefactor dreamed of creating a New Wales. Falkland's tract of land on the Avalon Peninsula was sandwiched between that of Baltimore's on the north and Vaughan's to the south.

Falkland bought another parcel of land at the same time from the London and Bristol Company that was the Bonavista Peninsula of the island. In applying to the king for his grant, Falkland listed his reasons for wanting to establish a plantation as "...For the Honour of God and the king; that part of the Country is not inhabited; His Majesty's undoubted right to the Country; that the London [and Bristol Company] Plantation has been settled for 13 years (Guy's Colony); the Bristol Plantation 5 years; and Lord Baltimore's the two years last past; the advantages — Trade from Ireland to Newfoundland."

Carey and some associates formed the Dublin Company and operated from his South Falkland colony on the Avalon Peninsula. It seems his purpose was strictly commerce although he touted other more philanthropic reasons which Calvert also seemed to pursue. Falkland brought the first Irish settlers to Newfoundland in 1624 in an attempt to settle his South Falkland colony at the harbour of Renews. It is thought he sent out as many as 200 Irish youngsters that year.

He enticed them with an offer that: "Any labourer with capital who is willing to go to the plantation in person should receive an annual wage and 100 acres of land after five years residence...." Falkland got support for his project not only from Irish investors but also from English merchants. Even though he had the support of Vaughan and his governor, Sir Richard Whitbourne, Falkland's effort suffered economic collapse within three years.

In 1628 other adventurers encouraged him to try again, but Falkland had had enough. Most of his Irish youngsters returned home, but many stayed on to disperse into the surrounding coves to found many of the communities that still survive on the Shore today. Falkland concentrated his next effort on his northern colony of North Falkland on the Bonavista Peninsula. His now governor, Whitebourne, had more success there than Carey had had on the Avalon Peninsula. The chief settlement at Bonavista went on to become one of the major fishing and commercial centres in Newfoundland.

Overall however, the plantations of James I were considered to be failures. Only two of their overseers - Guy and Calvert - ever actually went out to the country and neither stayed more than a year or so. The plantations failed as commercial ventures for a number of reasons: major among them being bad management. The absentee landlords relied on their governors who in many cases were looking out for their own best interests and not those of their benefactors. The competition of the merchant companies and the age-old rights of the Fishing Admirals led to disputes and lawlessness. A fishing captain had to pay as much as 200 pounds to rent two fishing rooms in the same harbour for the same season.

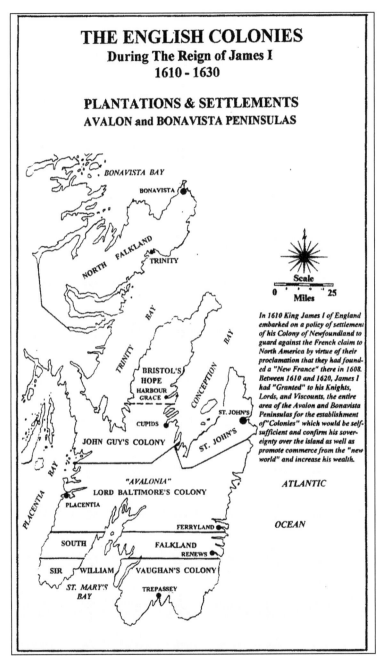

THE ENGLISH COLONIES
During The Reign of James I
1610 - 1630

PLANTATIONS & SETTLEMENTS
AVALON and BONAVISTA PENINSULAS

BONAVISTA BAY

BONAVISTA

NORTH FALKLAND

TRINITY

BAY

TRINITY

BAY

CONCEPTION BAY

BRISTOL'S HOPE

HARBOUR GRACE

CUPIDS

ST. JOHN'S

JOHN GUY'S COLONY

ST. JOHN'S

Scale
0   25
Miles

In 1610 King James I of England embarked on a policy of settlement of his Colony of Newfoundland to guard against the French claim to North America by virtue of their proclamation that they had founded a "New France" there in 1608. Between 1610 and 1620, James I had "Granted" to his Knights, Lords, and Viscounts, the entire area of the Avalon and Bonavista Peninsulas for the establishment of "Colonies" which would be self-sufficient and confirm his sovereignty over the island as well as promote commerce from the "new world" and increase his wealth.

"AVALONIA"
LORD BALTIMORE'S COLONY

PLACENTIA

PLACENTIA BAY

SOUTH

FERRYLAND

FALKLAND

RENEWS

SIR WILLIAM

VAUGHAN'S COLONY

ST. MARY'S BAY

TREPASSEY

ATLANTIC

OCEAN

The English Colonies — During the Reign of James I (Map: B.F.)

Some are of the opinion that the settlers picked to work the plantations simply were not up to the task. According to one observer, the Irish colonizers of Falkland were no better suited to the task than were Vaughan's Welshmen. Falkland's "colonists were like the uncivilized Welsh brought out by Wynne; it was the custom of the age to capture men for all kinds of service, and in all probability Vaughan's settlers and Falkland's colonists were simply corralled like so many cattle and sent out to the new settlement. There was no practical farmer to teach them how to clear the land; they were green hands and no help at the fishery; it is no marvel therefore...that they were failures; these causes, combined with the want of a practical, energetic, experienced man at the head of affairs, fully explains why these aristocratic schemes to colonize Newfoundland did not succeed."

Yet the failure was only from the mercantile point of view. All of the colonies that established a settlement went on to survive as fishing communities — Guy's Cupids, Vaughan's Trepassey, Falkland's Renews and Bonavista, and Calvert's Ferryland. All survive today, if not as thriving fishing centres at least as viable ones. Around the plantation hubs there grew a scattering of outports, many of which still exist today.

Of these grandiose schemes for settlement of Newfoundland, historian D.W. Prowse commented: "We can admire the enthusiasm that set them on foot, the eloquent language with which they were recommended to the public.... [But].... Not a vestige of these colonies remain; all the fantastic names of New Falkland, Cambriol Colchos, Vaughan's Cove, Britanniola etc., with the one exception of Baltimore's Avalon, have disappeared from the maps..."

These schemes, Prowse went on, "had elaborate Charters prepared in the chambers of Kings, princes and potentates lent the weight of their names and dignity to these great state documents; they offered court barons, court leet, and territorial agrandisement [sic] to their associates...and these fantastic titles and aristocratic forms...faded and died away in the rude free air of the Colonies. None of the great patentees from Gilbert to Baltimore, exercised the least permanent influence on the history of the Colony..."

In the final analysis it was not the "aristocratic and fantastic patentees" who settled and colonized Newfoundland, but the hard-working settlers and fishermen from West Country England and Ireland, many of who fled here to escape hardship in their homelands only to find much the same in Newfoundland, yet persevered long after the belted lords and barons had given up.

CHAPTER II

Baltimore's Folly

In 1621 King James I of England embarked on a quest to form an alliance with Spain to counter the growing strength of his latest adversary — France. To secure this alliance he proposed to King Philip III of Spain that his son Charles wed his daughter Maria, the *infantada princess*. To woe Philip, James chose one of his most able and trusted courtiers, Sir George Calvert, to be his ambassador to the court of Spain.

Calvert embarked on what was to prove to be one of the most difficult — if not dangerous — tasks of his Royal service. The international political intrigues and machinations of the period were at the very least somewhat convoluted. Royalty ruled, and their word was law, divinely sanctioned and no question of motive or method was countenanced. Sir George, being a close confidant of James, no doubt knew well the nuances and eccentricities of the king.

James was not a popular pick of the English people for their sovereign. He had reluctantly been named heir to the throne by his autocratic aunt, Elizabeth I of England who had his mother — who was her own sister — Mary Queen of Scots expeditiously beheaded. Two years after he ascended the throne English Catholics led by Guy Fawkes tried to blow him up in the infamous gunpowder plot. James had extravagant, lavish, and expensive habits and tastes, all of which served to alienate him from his subjects. By 1620 he found his coffers nearly empty and looked for ways to replenish them.

It may have been this need for money that led him to his liberal permissions to the entrepreneurs who petitioned him for grants to establish plantations in Newfoundland and Virginia where some of them were convinced that the streets were literally paved with gold. Vaughan in particular had convinced the king with his books the *Golden Fleece* and *Cambriol Colchos*, or "Golden Grove" as he called his New Wales, which he pointed out had existed for three years by 1620 "without any such mortal accidents." James was not a well man physically by now and his affliction may have at times clouded his judgment. It is believed he suffered from the "royal family disease," porphyria, the same debilitating condition that is thought to have caused the madness of King George III a hundred years later. Indeed, it is thought that James I introduced the disease into the royal family of England.

James had other "afflictions" also: one of them his proclivity for young men which he surrounded himself with at his royal court. It is not believed that Calvert was one of his favourite fellows, but one who was, George Villiers, a one-time royal cup-bearer later titled the Duke of Buckingham by the king, was to be a character of some import in Calvert's chore over the coming few years.

It was openly joked in London after James first came to the throne upon the death of Queen Elizabeth that: "Elizabeth was King: now James is Queen." James had a family: his wife was Anne of Denmark, and they had three children — the eldest, his daughter Elizabeth was said to be a beautiful girl; Henry his eldest son was referred to as a promising boy, and Charles who was noted as a rather delicate child. James was said to have commented quite frankly once that: "You may be sure that I love the Duke of Buckingham more than anyone else..." As James put it: "Jesus had his John, I have my George."

The king was also known to be very open-handed with less intimate friends and hangers-on at court. Not being one of James's favourite fellows, and given his position at court, Calvert probably fell into the category of less intimate friends rather than hangers-on.

James I. He began the period of colonization in Newfoundland and the New World in the early 1600s which saw several attempts by entrepreneurs and romantics like Lord Baltimore try to establish "plantations" in Newfoundland as well as on the mainland of America. Although none of them succeeded on the island as commercial ventures, they did establish an English presence and a thriving fishery from Newfoundland which resulted in many of the initial plantations becoming viable and profitable settlements that survived the centuries. (Photo: *Wikipedia* [PD-Public Domain].)

In 1621, the same year that Calvert sent out his first contingent of colonizers to Avalonia, he undertook his first trip to Spain as James's ambassador to try to arrange the royal marriage. He was to make several trips in the attempt which lasted for extended periods and was probably the reason he did not visit his colony sooner than he did.

Calvert's efforts to arrange the marital treaty were thwarted by the bonnie Prince Charles himself. Destined to become the next King of England due to his brother's early death, Charles became impatient with Calvert's diplomacy and sought his father's permission to pursue the matter on his own behalf.

Charles was now about twenty years of age and decided to travel to Spain disguised as the female companion of James's favourite fellow, the Duke of Buckingham. In Spain they met the Princess Maria who seemed to prefer the company of the "female" companion of the Duke. In a romantic interlude Charles was revealed to be a prince indeed and the infuriated Princess proclaimed that she would rather go into a convent than marry a heretic and go live in a heathen country. Charles returned to England with a definite "no" to his father's plans.

Calvert's job as matchmaker was finished. What he had tried to accomplish by four years of diplomacy had fallen apart in one short visit by a fop of a true prince and a favourite fellow.

It was during these years in Spain that Calvert grasped the mettle to reaffirm his Catholic faith. He became acquainted with the Spanish Count Gondomar, the Spanish ambassador to the court of King James, and a close friend of Calvert's later confided that it was largely due to Gondomar's influence as well as the Baron Arundel of Wardour, another close confidant of King James, that Calvert decided to declare publicly his conversion to Catholicism.

The Baron Arundel came from a rich family near Wardour in the south of England, had extensive interests in the overseas colonies, and shared Calvert's views on establishing a religious haven for Catholics in America. Some years later Calvert's eldest son Cecil would wed Arundel's daughter Anne. Dogmatic religious persuasion and wealthy marital matchmaking aside, there may have been deeper reasons for Calvert's sudden pronouncement that he had converted to the Catholic faith.

Calvert had been born into a Catholic family during the reign of Elizabeth I who had declared herself head of the Church of England and English Protestantism in the 1570s. Calvert's parents were by the standards of the day wealthy people with title, land holdings and other property.

Although the Calverts did so publicly, they may not have renounced their Catholic faith privately. Sir George likely grew up indoctrinated and following the religious faith he was born into. Even while he was a confident of King James he showed an open concern and compassion for the plight of the persecuted English Catholics as their religion came under increasing attack as the Thirty Years War progressed. He was especially concerned about the treatment of the Irish Catholics in their homeland and it was probably during these years that he formulated his plans to create a safe haven for them in his imagined refuge of Avalonia.

During these years of reintroduction to the Catholic religion, Calvert also went through a period of personal turmoil and tragedy. Some accounts say that in 1622 his wife, Anne Mynne died, and two years later his eldest daughter expired. Other accounts dispute this saying that he and Anne were divorced around 1622. There may be some truth to the latter version. It is stated in some accounts that Calvert had a bastard son (Newfoundland historian D.W. Prowse is author of this statement) who other accounts identify as his second son Leonard, born in 1610. It is not known for certain who was Leonard's mother. Calvert's marriage was almost five years old by this time and his indiscretion may not have been a fleeting one. By 1622 Lady Calvert may have simply tired of his indiscretions if they continued.

It is also known that Calvert's second wife Lady Joan (or Joanne) had reportedly been the handmaiden of Lady Anne and nanny to the Calvert children. The first version is no doubt more palatable to Catholics of the period, or even today, but one can see the inferences one might conclude. The records do show that one of Calvert's daughters did die in 1624 but it was not his eldest daughter Ann but his second daughter Dorothy, born sometime in 1608 who died on January 13 of 1624.

Whichever the case, the same year that Calvert lost his wife he sent out a second contingent of settlers to his Newfoundland colony. They were led by Captain Daniel Powell and numbered 22 people, many of them the wives of the builders sent out with Wynn the previous year. Powell's group were to be the settlers who would populate and prosper the colony. Powell, like Wynn, was also a Welshman as were his colonizers. Calvert had not yet broached his scheme to send out his English and Irish Catholics.

Powell and his group were late in arriving at Ferryland due to bad weather which forced him to land at Bay Bulls twenty miles north of the colony. It was late July by the time he wound his way down the shore to Avalonia. During the rest of the summer he spent his time exploring the coves and bays nearby and reported to Calvert that he had located a couple of suitable coves for the expansion of the colony.

He wrote Calvert requesting even more people and resources to establish a second settlement which he suggested would "...give comfort and help to the present Plantation, and quickly ease your Honour's charge, if a Plantation be there this next Spring settled. If therefore it will please your Honour to let me be furnished against that time, but with thirteen men, and give me leave to settle my selfe [sic] there, I make no doubt...but to give your Honour, and the rest of the undertakers such content, that you shall have good encouragement to proceed further therein."

Later developments seem to suggest that Wynn and his lieutenant, Powell, conspired to make themselves rich at Calvert's expense. Wynn wrote Sir George later in the year also requesting further assistance. He wanted more men, including six masons, four carpenters, two or three "Quarry men, a Slater [rock cutter] or two, a Lyme-burner and Lyme stones, a good quantity of strong laths, a couple of strong maids, that besides other work can brew and bake and weave hemp and flax, and a convenient number of West Countrey labourers to fit the ground for the Plough."

He also wanted a Gunner and cannons and "A complete Magazine of requirements." He complained that although he acquired 186 hogsheads of salt from masters at "Formose" (Fermuse) and "Renouze" (Renews), that "some did not like our flourishing beginning." He also complained about the transient fishermen who yearly visited the nearby outports and had "rinded this year not so few as 50,000 trees and they heave out ballast in the harbours."

Calvert's scheme for settlement, sponsored by the Newfoundland Company, a subsidiary of the waning London and Bristol Company, was diametrically opposed to the policies of the West Country Merchants Company which wanted no permanent settlement on the island. They wanted only a seasonal fishery from Newfoundland and all the proceeds returning to England and their pockets.

The masters whom Wynn and Powell mentioned in their reports to Calvert were the Fishing Admirals of the West Country Merchants who in later years would rule with their word as the law. They ruthlessly controlled every harbour and cove where men went to "make fish."

During the winter of 1622–23, Wynn and Powell built a wharf in Ferryland harbour — probably in the area of the "Pool," the most sheltered spot of the otherwise open port. Their "brewe house," forge and saltworks were also completed and in the spring of 1623 Wynn sent off a barrel "of the best salt that ever my eyes beheld" to his landlord in London. Wynn also informed Calvert of his intention to "enlarge this little roome [meaning the cove or bay where men fished] so that within the same, for the comfort of neighbor-hood another row of buildings may be so pitched so that the whole may be a prettie street.... For the country and climate; it is better and not so cold as England.... Wee have prospered to the admiration of all the beholders in what is done."

It seems that both Wynn and Powell expected Calvert to be another of the belted barons of absentee landlords like Vaughan and Falkland, and were trying to milk him for all they could get. Powell's suggestion that he could start a second settlement at "Caplin Bay, which would give comfort and help to the present Plantation," got financial support from Calvert and survives today as a community later renamed for him.

By now, Calvert had invested a large sum of money in his adventure and could not afford to let his colony fail. In addition to the opposition of the West Country Merchants he also had to contend with the competition of his own allies. Lord Falkland had planted himself right at his back door and was trying to revive Vaughan's failed settlement of three or four years earlier at Renews.

Despite his personal losses and stresses, Calvert remained diligent to his duties to the king, at least outwardly. When James became embroiled with Parliament in a controversy over the right of the plantation grantees to tax independent "ship-fishermen" on their cargoes and forbid their ships entry into any port along the English coast if the taxes weren't forthcoming, Calvert sided with the king, for obvious reasons — he himself was a plantation owner.

The "independent" fishermen brought their case before Parliament and Calvert in his capacity as Secretary of State argued for King James that: "America is not annexed to the realm; it is a plantation solely governed by the Crown." This stand of the Crown proved to be very unpopular with the common folk of England, since they were the "independent" fishermen involved, and eventually led to the downfall of the monarchy in the bloody civil wars under the reign of Charles I twenty years later.

In 1624 Calvert suddenly announced his conversion to Catholicism and was promptly denounced as a popist; the reaction of most of his colleagues on the Privy Council was not very favourable. He resigned his position as the King's Secretary of State since James could not tolerate such a public affront but the king retained him on the Privy Council. Calvert also surrendered his Manor Estate in Longford, Ireland when he refused to accept the king's condition that all his people there "should be comfortable in point of religion," meaning they should be loyal Anglicans.

Calvert was still an influential person however and to avoid public confrontation James rewarded his long-time confidant and loyal servant by elevating him to the Irish Peerage as Baron Baltimore of County Longford and awarded him a 2,000 pound a year pension. Why Calvert chose the name Baltimore for his title is unclear, since the name came from a small hamlet on the south coast of Ireland in what would become the County of Cork in the Province of Munster. His titled land at Longford was located in north-central Ireland in what would later become County Longford in the province of Leinster, quite some distance away. When he retired from James's court in 1625 he went to live on a large estate he owned in County Wexford, Ireland and was never known to have lived on his Manor Estate in Longford. He also maintained a home in London during these years where he spent most of his time while he tried to establish his colony in Newfoundland.

Calvert had planned to visit his Colony of Avalonia in 1624 but the death of his daughter delayed his plans. His subsequent grief, which some claim led him to proclaim his conversion to Catholicism, and his forced resignation from the king's service further delayed his plans. He may also have been prompted to visit his colony for other reasons.

In 1624 a close friend, Sir William Alexander, also in the king's court and an entrepreneur interested in the colonies, returned from a tour of the plantations in Newfoundland and reported to James in a short treatise titled *An Encouragement To Colonies*, in which he gave an evaluation of their progress.

Of his friend Calvert's Avalonia, he wrote that he had for "both building and making trail of ground has done more than ever was performed by any other in so short a time, having already there a broode [sic] of Horses, Kowes, and other beastial, and by the industry of his people he is beginning to draw back yearly some benefit from thence already."

Despite his official report, Alexander reported to Calvert that although he was gaining "some benefit from thence" he could be gaining more. In the words of Alexander "Wynn had contrived to make some appearance of profit [for himself]...but was prevented." Alexander intimated that Wynn and Powell had "so plundered the unsuspecting Baltimore that he at last had to visit the colony to look after his interests." The complicated factors that figured in Calvert's life between 1621 and 1625 delayed his plans time after time but left him with the urgency to go see for himself.

By 1625 King James had died and his "delicate" son Charles had ascended the throne as Charles I, James's eldest "promising" son Henry having died before his father. Charles knew the influence Calvert had on and dependence his father had shown in the former Privy Council member and Secretary of State, and tried to woo him back into his fold. He restored Calvert's Longford Estate to him and offered to dispense with the oath of religious supremacy for his settlers if Calvert would stay in his Privy Council, but the Lord Baltimore declined the offer.

Charles I. Charles succeeded his father James I to the throne of England in 1625. It was during his later reign that Lord Baltimore, who had worked for years to "arrange" his marriage to the Spanish Princess, that Calvert's claim to Avalonia would be usurped by Sir David Kirke and upheld by Charles. (Photo: Prowse — 1895.)

In 1626 Calvert decided he must go across to his Avalonia. He quickly found that many of his former colleagues in council and state had become religious bigots and not friends indeed. As he attempted to ready his expedition to his colony he found himself being blocked by many of his former friends in both the king's court and in Parliament. By March of that year he had contracted for two ships and crews to transport him to Newfoundland along with a further contingent of colonists and a herd of cattle to further strengthen his settlement.

His opponents succeeded in frustrating his plans however when they had his hired ships conscripted into the king's service. Calvert wrote one of his influential friends in the House of Lords, Lord Coke, requesting him to intercede on his behalf. "I intend shortly," Calvert wrote Coke, "God willing, a journey to Newfoundland to visit a plantation I have begun there some years since. I hired the ship called *Jonathan* now in the River for the transport of myself and such planters as I carry with me. But I understand that she is stayed for the King so I must give place. But I am by that means utterly disappointed and you should do me the duty to clear her and her mariners and also the *Peter Bonaventure* for which I contracted for carrying cattle."

★ Kiplin: Birthplace of Sir George Calvert, First Lord Baltimore — 1582.

◉ Oxford: Site of Trinity College where Calvert received his education.

✱ London: Calvert lived here during his years in King James's service and maintained a home there until his death in 1632.

▣ Wardour: Probable site of Calvert's Conversion to Catholicism under the auspices of his friend Baron Arundell.

● Longford: Site of Calvert's plantation granted to him by James I upon his retirement.

✪ Baltimore: Namesake of Calvert's chosen Title.

Map — Calvert Country. (Map: B.F.)

Calvert was eventually able to get his contracted ships released but only with the proviso that his expedition did not remain any longer than ten days in Newfoundland for the purpose of landing his people and cattle, and that the ships return with a cargo of salt fish to supply the Royal Navy. His anti-Catholic opponents confided to each other that "Baltimore...now a professed popist, was going to Newfoundland but is stayed."

The newly dubbed Lord Baltimore also had adversaries in his own back yard overseas. A Church of England clergyman who had been sent out to administer to the settlers of Vaughan's and Calvert's colonies was not pleased that Baltimore might be planning a haven for Catholics in the New World.

The Reverend Erasmus Stourton was the first Church of England clergyman to be sent to the Newfoundland plantations with John Guy's expedition in 1610 and by 1625 was considered the head cleric of the Church in the colonies on the island. He was to be the instigator of much aggravation for Calvert in the coming years and may have begun it even before Calvert arrived in his colony.

When news reached Newfoundland that Calvert intended to visit his colony and investigate reports about his governors, Wynn decided to resign his position, citing as reasons ill health and old age. As he informed Baltimore: "I am now full of years and travails..." Calvert soon found himself a new governor however, one he felt he could trust, Sir Arthur Aston who was also a Catholic, and he was successful in having him sail with 15 Catholic settlers to Ferryland, "so that they might begin to establish the church there...." Aston spent a year in Ferryland and upon his return informed Calvert of the situation of his colony. Again, Baltimore was not pleased with the reports and became even more determined to visit his plantation in person.

In May of 1627 he petitioned the Secretary of State, Sir Thomas Wentworth to have the ships necessary to sail to Newfoundland despite the restrictions that had been placed on shipping because of the latest war between England and France. "It imports me more than in Curiosity only to see," Calvert wrote, "for I must go and settle it in a better order than it is, or else give it over and lose all Charges I have been at hitherto for other men to build their Fortunes upon. And I had rather been esteemed a fool by some for the Hazard of one month's Journey, than to prove myself one certainly for six years by past, if the business now be lost for want of a little pain and care."

PROFILE — "Mansion Manor": Baltimore's House

Lord Baltimore's governor, Captain Edward Wynn wrote him in 1621 that he had constructed a habitation he called the Governor's Residence which he said he had constructed mostly from stone. The residence was 44 feet long and 15 feet wide and consisted of a hall, a cellar, a stone kitchen and chimney, and a chamber over it consisting of four rooms — probably bedrooms. The only contemporary map that locates the Mansion Manor is the *Fitzhugh Map* of 1693 which was drawn some 70 years after the establishment of the Colony of Avalonia and the beginnings of the settlement of Ferryland.

The *Fitzhugh Map* claims to clearly shows the location of the governor's house as built by Captain Wynn in 1621 and later occupied by Lord Baltimore. Clearly labelled as "the Fort" (numbered 1 on the Map), it suggests that it was the main house of the tiny settlement surrounded by the seven-foot-high "palizado" as Wynn described it to Calvert in his report of 1622. It also shows that at the time of the map's draft the settlement of Ferryland consisted of several more dwellings strung out along the "Downs" (numbered 2 on Map), the "prettie little street" Wynn described to him.

Captain Powell who arrived a year after Wynn reported that the Governor's House was: "strong and well contrived, standeth very warm, at the foote of an easie ascending hill, on the South-east, and defended with a hill, standing on the further side of the Haven on the North-west; The Beach on the North and South sides of the Land locke it, and the seas on both sides are so neere and indifferent to it that one may shoot a Bird-bolt into either Sea. No cold can offend it, although it bee accounted the coldest Harbour in the Land, and the Seas doe make the land behind it to the South-east, being neere 1,000 acres of good ground for hay, feeding of Cattle, and plenty of wood, almost an island, safe to keepe anything from ravenous beasts."

The *Fitzhugh Map — 1693*. This Map drawn twenty years after the Dutch raid of 1673 and three years before the French raid of 1696 clearly shows the "governor's house" as being located at the foot of the "easie hill" that levels out into the "Downs." (Photo: Map from Prowse — 1895.)

The "almost an island" Powell referred to was likely the Downs as it has come to be called, seen on *Fitzhugh's Map* with the row of houses extending out to Ferryland Head.

Some investigators think that the house was constructed completely from wood except for the fireplaces and chimneys, while others believe the entire outer wall was constructed of stone. The Dutch destroyed the house in 1673 but it was likely reconstructed by the widow Kirke who was still proprietor of the governor's property at that time. It was destroyed again, burned or cannon-balled by the French raid of de Brouillon in 1696-97. It has been speculated that over the next century or so any stone remaining from the building was probably utilized by settlers to make fireplaces, chimneys, build walls, or for any number of other practical purposes.

Sketches of both the floor plans and exterior facade of Lord Baltimore's Mansion Manor were hypothetically proposed by Dr. R.A. Barakat of the Department of Anthropology of Memorial University of Newfoundland some thirty years ago. Barakat based his speculations and drawings on the first-hand account of Baltimore's governor Wynn. In a letter to Calvert written by Wynn from Ferryland on August 17, 1622, Wynn reported: "...the building being 44 foote of length & 15 foote of breadth, and containing a hall 18 foote long, an entry of six foote and a cellar of 20 foote in length, and of the height between the ground floore and that over the head about 8 foote, being divided above that throughout into foure chambers, and foure foote high to the roofe or a half storie. The roofe over the hall I covered with deale boards and the rest with such thatch as I found...being a far better covering...both for warmth and liteness. When I had finished the frame with onely one Chimney of stone work in the hall, I went forward with our kitchen, of a length of 18 foote, 12 foote of breadth, and 8 foote high to the eves, and walled up with stonework with a Chimney in the frame. Over the Kitchen I fitted another Chamber. All which with a staircase and convenient passages, both into the Kitchen and the rooms over it were all finished by Christmas Eve."

The exact location of Baltimore's Mansion Manor as of 2005 has not been definitely pinpointed. The common consensus today is that it was located somewhere in the Pool area. The *Fitzhugh Map* clearly shows it to be west of the Downs on a gentle slope that overlooks the Pool and Ferryland Harbour. If so, the Mansion Manor remains may lie beneath the present-day parish hall and main highway through Ferryland. Dr. James Tuck of the archaeology unit of Memorial University who has been digging for the site for the last decade or so believes he is close to finding it in the Pool area very near the Kirke House.

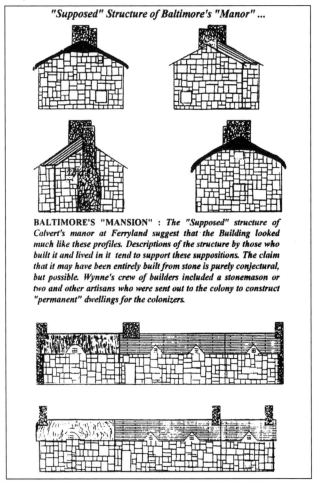

"Supposed" Structure of Baltimore's "Manor" ...

BALTIMORE'S "MANSION" : *The "Supposed" structure of Calvert's manor at Ferryland suggest that the Building looked much like these profiles. Descriptions of the structure by those who built it and lived in it tend to support these suppositions. The claim that it may have been entirely built from stone is purely conjectural, but possible. Wynne's crew of builders included a stonemason or two and other artisans who were sent out to the colony to construct "permanent" dwellings for the colonizers.*

The "Supposed Structure" of Calvert's Mansion Manor at Ferryland suggests that the building looked much like these profiles. Descriptions of the structure by those who built it and lived in it tend to support these suppositions. The claim that it may have been entirely built from stone is purely conjecture, but possible. Wynn's crew of builders included a stonemason or two sent out to the colony to construct permanent dwellings for the colonizers. (Sketches after Barakat — 1973.)

In 2003 Dr. Tuck commented that: "...we could say that just maybe we've found the Mansion House.... Unfortunately, the house lies under the road that runs from the community of Ferryland out to the lighthouse.... So for now we have to say that maybe we've found the Mansion House, but we'll have to wait for more excavations to be certain of just who lived in this house and exactly when it was built in the first place."

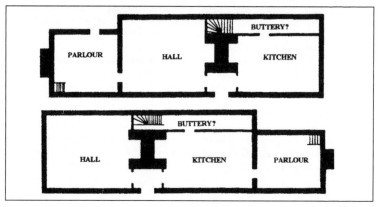

"Supposed" Floor Plans of Baltimore's "Mansion Manor" showing chimney locations.

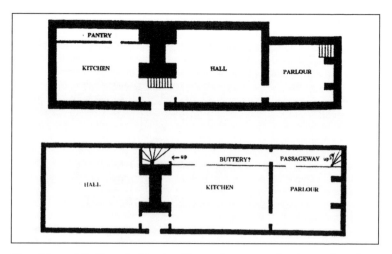

Floor Plans of Baltimore's Mansion Manor also suggest that it may have been "expanded" by later occupants, probably the Kirkes, which some accounts report saw the house looking like a veritable castle complete with towers. (Sketches after Barakat — 1973.)

And so the search goes on today as archaeologists continue to dig and search for the remnants of what was the first Mansion Manor to be built in Newfoundland almost 400 years ago.

The Pool and Downs at Ferryland around the turn of the twentieth century. The descriptions from Calvert's governors Wynn and Powell in the early 1620s suggest that Baltimore's Mansion Manor was located just below the gentle slope of the hill at centre bottom of picture. (Photo: MUN-CNS.)

CHAPTER III

Baltimore's *Avalonia*

𝕎here James I had been at least tolerant, and even grateful for Calvert's service and loyalty, Charles I proved to be more difficult to deal with. The new king probably still smarted from his rejection by the Spanish Princess Maria and may have blamed Calvert for his "missed" match. Charles had also inherited many of his father's councillors, some of whom had become adversaries of Calvert following his conversion to Catholicism. Lord Baltimore persisted however, and in 1627 finally travelled to his Colony of Avalonia. He set sail on June 1 and arrived in Ferryland on July 23. For a summer crossing it was a long voyage and may have been a harbinger of things to come.

With him Baltimore had brought two Catholic priests, Father Thomas Longville, son of the Knighted Lord, Sir Henry Longville, and the other a middle-class Londoner, Father Anthony Pole, who travelled under the rather conspicuous alias of Smith. Once landed Calvert wasted no time in beginning his crusade.

Baltimore's priests blessed his landing and his colony by celebrating the first Roman Catholic mass to be held in a British possession in North America. Calvert's colony by now numbered about 100 souls, about one quarter of them Catholics who had come out with his new governor, Aston, the previous year.

Calvert found that he indeed did have a large and comfortable Manor House which was "strong and well contrived." He immediately began to hear glowing accounts from his colonists as well as those in Vaughan's and Falkland's settlements of the bounties of the country. Most importantly, he heard that fish was in abundance and the price was high since the recent war between England and France had begun.

Vaughan's planters told of "three men in 30 days catching fish worth — with oil, 160 pounds." Game too, was plentiful. "One man near Renoos [Renews]," he was told, "killed 700 partridges." Others told of the "numerous deer" [caribou] to be found but a few short miles inland, and more told that you "have there faire Strawberries red and white, and as faire Raspberrie, and Gooseberries as there are in England; and also multitudes of Billberries...and many other delicate Berries...in great abundance."

Baltimore found another thing to be in great abundance — the religious prejudice that he was seeking to escape in England. The Reverend Stourton, who considered himself the head of the Church of England in the colonies of Newfoundland, railed at Calvert when he heard that the Catholic mass had been celebrated at Ferryland. He vehemently protested Baltimore's popish practices, but when Baltimore persisted, allowing both Anglican and Catholic services to be conducted under the same roof — his own house, Stourton complained to the king.

In reply, Calvert invoked the full rights of his grant which gave him absolute power and rule over his colony. Provisions of his grant gave him "civil rights as full as the Bishop of Durham." Durham at that time was the last of the medieval *palatinates*, and as Lord Palantine, Baltimore was invested with absolute civil and ecclesiastical authority with the power to appoint and dismiss clergymen. He promptly dismissed Stourton.

The Reverend Stourton returned to England where he poured out complaints of his treatment at the hands of the popist Baltimore and warned of Calvert's designs to encourage Popery on His Majesty's English subjects in Ferryland. He swore out a deposition to the Privy Council in which he declared that: "My Lord Baltimore...brought with him...seminary priests...who every Sunday say the Masse and doe profess all other of the ceremonies of the Church of Rome in the ample manner as tis used in Spayne. And this deponent hath seen them at Masse and knoweth that the child of one William Poole, a Protestant, was baptized according to the orders and customs of the Church of Rome by the procurement of the said Lord Baltimore contrary to the will of the said Poole to which childe the said Lord was a witness."

Stourton's rancour was venomous but Baltimore's rights under his grant patent were considered inviolate. Calvert stayed only about ten weeks in Ferryland then returned to London close on the heels of Stourton to answer the charges he knew would be brought against him. All that winter Calvert defended himself against Stourton's charges in both the king's court and Parliament, and both the king and Parliament — whatever their biases — could not deny the democratic rights they were obliged to uphold by their very existence. Stourton's complaints were deemed to be unfounded and Calvert was allowed to follow his plans as he wished.

By now Lord Baltimore had decided to take up permanent residence in his colony. Some accounts say that he left England with his entire family except his oldest son Cecilus (Cecil) while others say he took "most of his family" except Cecil who stayed behind to look after family affairs in

England. Cecil may have remained behind for other reasons. By now Calvert had remarried and the latest Lady Calvert, Joane (or Joanne) travelled with the latest member of the Calvert family, baby Philip who had been born on March 20, 1628. If this account is accurate then they made the Atlantic crossing with an infant child of only some two or three months of age given that he is reported to have arrived in Newfoundland in June of 1628.

It is known that he brought at least some of his children with him. Some accounts say he was also accompanied by two sons-in-law but accounts from history of the later Maryland Colony dispute that he had two at the time. His eldest daughter, Ann had married one William Peasely in 1627 and his fourth daughter Grace, said to have arrived with the second son-in-law, Sir Robert Talbot, is not recorded as having been married until 1630 in Kildare County, Ireland. It is quite possible however that they arrived as a betrothed couple. Some confusion arises when the records also show that his youngest daughter, Helen, born in 1619 also later married a James Talbot (whether related to the first Talbot or not is unknown) but she would have been only nine years of age at the time.

Of his eleven children by his first marriage to Anne Mynne, by now at least two and possibly three had died. His second eldest daughter, Dorothy, as well as his tenth child and sixth and last son by his first wife, John had died in infancy in February 1618. Another daughter, the third, Elizabeth had been born in 1609 and her death date is unknown. If all the family except Cecil and the deceased ones made that journey with him then he had at least eight and possibly nine of his sons and daughters with him on the trip. In any event there was a fine crowd of Calverts that crossed the Atlantic that summer of 1628.

Baltimore also brought another priest, one Father Hackett — also believed to be an alias for one Anthony Whitehaur (or Whitehair) — with him to replace Father Longville who had returned with him the previous year, and 40 more Roman Catholic colonists.

He had barely arrived and landed his baggage when French privateers attacked his colony. The French buccaneers, under the famous, or infamous, Marquis de la Rade, had been raiding all the English fishing stations along the coast of the Avalon Peninsula for more than a year and Calvert determined to put a stop to their raids. He reported to England that during the summer "a French Man-of-War...one Monsieur de la Rade of Dieppe who, with three ships and 400 men well armed and appointed came into my harbour of Cape Broile (Broyle), where he surprised divers of the fishermen, took two of their ships in the harbour and kept possession of them until I sent two ships of mine with some 100 men being all the force we could make upon the suddayne in this place where I am planted..."

He commandeered a Royal Navy man-o'-war on station in the area and with his own ship went in pursuit of the French "pirates." He caught up to them in Cape Broyle harbour and reported that the French ships "were much better of saile" and eluded him. He did recover the English ships and took 67 of the Frenchmen prisoners who had been left behind by the French ships in their haste to escape.

Calvert was determined to have some retribution on the French for the damage they had done to his fishery and his small outports. As he put it: "Hereupon still being vexed with these men (and both myselfe and my poore fisherie here and many others of your Majesty's subjects much injured this yeere by them) I directed my warship in consort with Captain Fearne's Man O' War...to seek out some of that nation at Trepasse, a harbour to the south where they used to fish."

Baltimore found that the French still fished there. His pair of ships found six French vessels in the harbour at Trepassey: five from *Bayonne* and one from *St. Jean de Luc*. The Frenchmen at first showed fight but with no chance of escape they surrendered after a brief exchange of cannon fire and Baltimore captured them along with "their lading of fish and trayne [oil] and [I] have sent them to England." He also sent the French crews to England as prisoners of war even though an uneasy truce had recently been struck between the two countries.

During the autumn, Calvert and his newly landed family all settled into the governor's house at Ferryland. The quarters would have been somewhat cramped for two (or three) married couples, a handful of young men and women and two celibate priests, but Calvert thought they could manage for the winter as he planned to expand the Manor in the spring.

The congestion was somewhat relieved when Calvert sent his son Leonard back to England with the captured French prizes and prisoners along with a report of the French privateer de la Rade's raid, and a request that the king send him two warships to protect the English fishery along the coast of the Avalon Peninsula.

When Leonard Calvert reached there Lord Baltimore found that he was engulfed in another controversy with English merchants who wanted to claim restitution for the damages done their businesses in Newfoundland and figured they should have that restitution out of Calvert's booty.

Baltimore believed he was at least entitled to two of the French prize ships which he hoped to use as the warships he wanted. But he was awarded only one, the *St. Claude* that was returned under command of his son with the understanding that it was to be "lent for twelve months only." Calvert could only have thought that his colonizing attempt was being contested and blocked at every turn.

He wrote bitter letters of complaint to both the king and his long-time and influential friend, the Duke of Buckingham. After thanking the king profusely for sending him the loan of a ship, he complained of "the malice and calumny of those who seek to make [him] appear foul in His Majesty's eyes," and "those who go about to supplant and destroy me are persons notoriously lewd and wicked. Such a one is that knave, Stourton...that audacious man who did last wynter raise a false and slanderous report of me at Plymouth..."

To the Duke of Buckingham he commented: "I came to build, to settle, to sowe...but I am given to fighting with Frenchmen...." But all his further appeals to have a second ship sent out to him fell on deaf ears.

Baltimore's real troubles were just beginning. The reports of the mild winters that his colony had been experiencing in the last seven years suddenly seemed to have been greatly exaggerated. The winter of 1628–29 swept in on his colony with a vengeance. It was to be one of the worst winters in decades and began with bitterly cold, high winds and frequent snowfalls in early November of 1628.

For six long months the colony was battered by snow and sleet storms and raging blizzards. The cold was bitter in the drafty wood and stone rooms of the governor's Mansion House. Lady Baltimore, used to the comforts of the London Courts and a much milder climate complained woefully of the savage weather. She fell ill, probably with scurvy, and was thought to also be afflicted with arthritis or rheumatism that must have been greatly aggravated by the cold and damp. Lady Joane had been a handmaiden to Baltimore's first wife, Anne Mynne, and his two daughters.

She was used to a much gentler life and the rigours of the winter at Ferryland were to take a heavy toll on her.

As the terrible winter persisted food became short and nearly half the colonists became sick, most of them with scurvy. Conditions for the settlers in their own rudimentary houses were even worse than inside the governor's house so Baltimore opened it up as a hospital. At one point there were as many as 50 stricken settlers occupying it. Before the merciless winter was over almost a dozen settlers were dead, most from the scurvy.

Lady Joane (Joanne) Calvert. Lady Baltimore (depicted here in a twentieth century painting) begged her husband to send her to some warmer and more hospitable "clime" after their terrible winter of 1628–29 in Ferryland. (Photo: Courtesy of Michelle O'Connell, The Colony Cafe, Ferryland. Painting by Stewart Montgomerie.)

The pressures and effects of the winter on Lady Baltimore must have been overbearing and by spring she beseeched her husband to take her to some warmer and more hospitable climate. Indeed, Baltimore himself had had enough of his "promising" Avalonia and decided to send his wife and most of the younger members of his family to the Colony of Virginia in New England.

Once Lady Joane had departed for there, Calvert reported to the king his horrendous winter at Ferryland. On August 19, 1629 he wrote Charles I: "...after much suffrance in this woeful country, where with one intolerable winter we were almost undone.... It is now to be expressed with my pen what we have endured." He went on to decry the severe weather and lack of food "for no plant or vegetable thing appearing out of the earth until it be about the beginning of May, nor fish in the sea...." Describing the conditions he endured during the winter he wrote: "my house has been a hospital all this winter, of 100 persons 50 sick at a time, myself being one and nine or ten of them died. Here upon I have had strong temptations to leave all proceedings in plantations, and being much decayed in my strength to retire myself to my former quiet; but my inclination carrying me naturally to these kind of works, and not knowing how better to employ the poor remainder of my days than with other good subjects to further the best I may the enlarging of your Majesty's empire in this part of the world I am determined to commit this place to fishermen that are better able to encounter storms and hard weather, and to remove myself with some forty persons to your Majesty's dominion of Virginia, where if your Majesty will please to grant me a precinct of land with such privileges as the King your father my gracious master was pleased to grant me here, I shall endeavour to the utmost of my power to deserve it and pray for your Majesty's long and happy reign...." He concluded with his hope "to quit my residence here and shift to some warmer climate of this new world where the winters be shorter and less rigorous."

Charles I had not been a great admirer of Calvert's, possibly because of his Spanish sojourn, but since many of his court were still powerful friends of Baltimore he may have been obliged to treat the Lord in an unbiased way. His reply to Calvert however, was neither sympathetic nor encouraging.

BALTIMORE'S LETTER
To
King Charles I
August 19, 1629

This last page of Lord Baltimore's letter written to King Charles 1 in 1629 informing him of his intention to quit his Colony at Ferryland gives the details of the miserable winter he spent there. After decrying the severe weather and lack of food *"for no plant or vegetable thing appearing out of the earth until it be about the beginning of May, nor fish in the sea..."* he goes on to describe the conditions he endured and says that by *"much salt meat my house has been a hospital all this winter, of 100 persons 50 sick at a time, myself being one and nine or ten of them died. Hereupon I have had strong temptations to leave all proceedings in plantations, and being much decayed in my strength to retire myself to my former quiet; but my inclination carrying me naturally to these kind of works, and not knowing how better to employ the poor remainder of my days than with other good subjects to further the best I may the enlarging of your Majesty's empire in this part of the world I am determined to commit this place to fishermen that are better able to encounter storms and hard weather, and to remove myself with some forty persons to your Majesty's dominion of Virginia, where if your Majesty will please to grant me a precinct of land with such privileges as the King your father my gracious master was pleased to grant me here, I shall endeavor to the utmost of my power to deserve it and pray for your Majesty's long and happy reign as ...*

Your Majesty's most humble and
faithful subject and servant
Geo. Baltimore

Ferryland
19 August 1629

Author's transcript of Lord Baltimore's handwritten letter: The last page of Baltimore's letter to King Charles I in August 1629, details the harsh and harrowing winter he endured at his Ferryland settlement in 1628–29. In it he requested permission to remove his colony to some warmer clime such as Virginia in New England.

He answered Baltimore by saying that he did not think the climate was "too hard" but that Calvert was "too soft." He also ordered Baltimore to return home. Calvert may have suspected he would have been and by the time he received his cheeky reply from the king he had already packed up and sailed off to Virginia. He left the remainder of his settlers in Avalonia under the charge of Governor William Hill, probably to ensure that his claims there could not be revoked by reason of his having abandoned the colony completely.

The Virginians may have been warned that Baltimore was coming. The colonists there were mostly Puritans and Presbyterians who were themselves "protestant" within the Protestant Church of England, and while the Anglican Church showed some tolerance of Roman Catholicism, the Puritans were prepared to show almost none.

At Jamestown, Virginia, Calvert was refused permission to settle in the colony unless he swore the oath of supremacy to the Church of England. Baltimore offered to swear the Oath of Loyalty to the Crown of England but would not take the Oath of Supremacy which required he recognize the King of England as head of his church and renounce the Pope and Catholicism. Calvert would not renounce his Catholic faith as his father had been forced to do. This was not acceptable to Governor Harvey of Virginia and Baltimore was obliged to return to England to plead his case before King Charles.

Before leaving he spent a couple of weeks cruising the coast of New England northwards away from Virginia and investigated the country in the Chesapeake Bay area which he decided would make good territory in which to try to establish another colony in America. He left for England late in the year to take up his cause. Lady Joane and his younger family members were said to follow him home on some later ship, which some accounts say was lost at sea with all hands. Other accounts say that their children were sent on ahead of them and that it was only Lady Joane who was lost at sea following his departure for England. Again there is some disagreement as to this incident.

The records for the Colony of Maryland tell that Philip Calvert, presumably his son by Lady Joane, later married a Miss Anne Wolseley and returned to Maryland in 1657 and was appointed governor of the colony in 1660. In recent years a grave site was unearthed in a special burial plot in St. Mary's City, Maryland and the remains therein tested for identification. They were found to be those of Philip Calvert, his wife and infant child.

The account of Lady Joane's loss at sea would agree with the assertion stated in the first account, that Baltimore married for a third time. If so it would have to have been between 1630 and his death in 1632, leaving him to waste little time or grief on the loss of his latest wife. It appears however, that he did marry a third time. One account explains that: "Calvert fell under a cloud, accused perhaps unjustly of trying in an unprincipled way to rid himself of a third wife, a maid of one of his daughters." Calvert was said to have quickly agreed that he and the woman could not have contracted a valid marriage because old canon law of the Catholic Church considered they had a spiritual relationship which precluded their union, that being that his first wife Anne Mynne, had been the maid's godmother. At the time of his death in1632 no wife is mentioned in his will.

Back in England, Baltimore immediately began petitioning the king for a grant to establish another colony in America, this time in New England.

PROFILE — Planters and Pirates

The plantations of the Colony of Newfoundland, which was officially begun by Sir Humphrey Gilbert in 1583 and first practically established by John Guy in 1610, ran a gauntlet of problems from weather to isolation, lack of funding to lack of settlers, political intrigues to commercial competition. Perhaps their worst scourge however, was the raiding they suffered at the hands of the privateers and buccaneers of other countries who competed with England for the trade and riches of the New World. Even more were Englishmen themselves and they were first-class pirates all.

John Guy, who established the colony's first plantation at Cupids, was naturally the pirates' first target. Only a year after he had settled in, Guy complained to his backers in England that he had been plundered by brigands. He reported that the pirate who raided him had been at Harbour Grace "trimming and repairing his shipping, and hath taken munitions etc., together with about 100 men out of the bay; he proposeth to have 500 out of the land before he goeth." Guy went on to say the pirate "was lately at Saint John's, and is now, as far as I can learn, at Ferryland, where he taketh his pleasure; and thereabouts the rest are to meet him."

Sir William Vaughan, trying to establish his colony at Trepassey, reported in the same year that a buccaneer or pirate had taken 100 cannon and 1,500 "mariners" (fisherman) out of the Newfoundland colonies "to the great hurt of the Newfoundland plantations."

The brigand – "buccaneer" – pirate that Guy and Vaughan referred to was Peter Easton, one of the most infamous of all the pirates to cruise the north and south Atlantic. Easton was a gentleman of aristocratic birth who once enjoyed the favour of Royalty but then fell from grace with the sea of fortune. An Englishman, he began his career as a privateer under the reign of Queen Elizabeth who actively encouraged and rewarded any privateer or buccaneer who would plunder her Spanish rivals. As a young man Easton enjoyed great success under Elizabeth's rule but when her successor James I took the throne and negotiated a peace with Spain, Easton fell out of favour and out of work and so turned his hand to piracy. One of his main targets was to become his former country of employment.

Pirate Peter Easton. He was imagined to look much like this stereotypical version of the romantic, swashbuckling buccaneer of the early 1600s. (Photo: Library of Congress.)

Hunted off the coasts of Spain and Africa, which were his regular haunts, he turned his sails to America and the Spanish Main. He decided to make his headquarters in Newfoundland and set up his base of operations at Harbour Grace in Conception Bay. He built himself a small fort there then began cruising the coves and bays looking to recruit men for his fleet. It was during this time that he raided the fledgling colonies of the island.

Easton had crossed the Atlantic with ten ships, most of them frigate class size with twenty to thirty guns and needing crews of 80 to 100 men to be battle ready. Easton's own ship, the *Happy Adventure*, was the largest of his fleet, sported forty guns and needed up to 180 men to fully compliment her for action. The ship, contrary to stereotypical pirate ships did not fly the Jolly Roger or skull and crossbones from its mast, but flaunted the red cross of St. George — the flag of England — from its mainmast.

Easton had picked Newfoundland because of its closeness to the shipping routes of the north Atlantic. He planned to plunder the Spanish Plate Fleet as it returned home from the Caribbean laden with its treasures of gold from central America. But to do it he needed crews for his ships and he knew he could get them from among the many fishing ships that visited Newfoundland each year. And so the colonies of Guy and Vaughan became his targets to recruit sailors. Virtually any cove that sheltered a fishing ship was likely to be raided by him and the mariners there carried off to do his buccaneering.

When he returned after about a year or so of raiding the Spanish Main he found that French Basques had taken over his fort at Harbour Grace. He immediately ousted them in typical pirate fashion and landed his prize, a Spanish galleon, which he now plundered, scuttled and burned, in the harbour. Having reestablished his control of the harbour he decided to move his headquarters to Ferryland on the Southern Shore. The Shore, he thought, was the perfect setting for a pirate. It was situated on the most easterly coastline of the island, perfectly poised to intercept any shipping from Europe, had a harbour easily defended by the *Isle aux Bois*, a grand lookout from the "gaze" just above the harbour, and the Pool which made an excellent drydock.

Easton built himself a fine house at Fox Point and is said to have buried the treasure from the Spanish galleon he had scrapped at Harbour Grace somewhere in or near Ferryland at the mouth of a river. At Ferryland he became lord of the place and his word ruled. By 1614 he had sent off to King James to have a pardon granted him for his waywardness. Such could be arranged he was told, if one had the money. Easton had it and King James, always strapped for funds, granted it — not once but twice in return for Easton's generous bounties.

The "Pool" (hook-shaped area at centre) was the most sheltered cove of Ferryland harbour and was "reserved" for the pirate "governor's" ship and those of other "important" visitors. It was directly overlooked from the "Gaze" and gave a clear view beyond the "Downs" and Ferryland "Head" far out to sea to allow Easton plenty of time to set sail if danger approached. (Photo: Courtesy K. Mooney. *Southern Scenics.*)

Thinking he was no longer a hunted man, Easton set in motion his long planned ambush of the Spanish Plate fleet. That fall he intercepted the Spanish treasure fleet off the Azores with his fourteen-ship fleet and sunk all the Spanish ships save for the four that carried the treasure trove.

Easton then left Ferryland and retired to France where he adopted the title of Marquis of Savoy and is said to have lived rich. Estimates of his fortune in his day put it at about two million pounds, which would probably be about ten times that amount in today's money.

He had left Ferryland after his tenure as Pirate King having plundered from the English 100 ships with their cannons, plus munitions and provisions to the amount of 10,400 pounds. He had also taken over "500 fishermen of His Majesty's subjects from their honest trade of fishing...." While many of these men "taken from their honest trade" were "impressed," just as many were willing "draftees." From the French he had pirated 25 ships, "one great" ship from the Flemish, and 12 from the Portuguese.

Easton had left Ferryland and Newfoundland just in time. Unknown to him he was still a hunted man, King James perhaps hoping to pardon him one more time for one more lucrative bounty. Soon after he left the hunter showed up in the person of Sir Henry Mainwarring who had been hunting Easton for two years despite his pardon. But during the hunt, Mainwarring had turned to buccaneering himself. He was another aristocrat who was well connected with the English Crown and had been given license to track down pirates like Easton. When Sir Henry arrived in Ferryland and found his prey gone he decided to move in himself and take over the job of Pirate King He too, decided to refurbish his fleet of eight ships at the expense of the colonies and the Newfoundland fishermen. From late June to early September he raided and plundered in Newfoundland's waters.

"Captain Maneringe [Mainwarring]," one official reported, "with divers other captains arrived in Newfoundland the 4th of June having eight sails of warlike ships...from all the harbours whereof they commanded carpenters, maryners [fishermen], victuals, munitions.... Of every six maryners they take one,,, From the Portugal ships they took all their wine and other provisions save their bread; from a French ship in Harbour Grace they took 10,000 fish; some of the company of many ships did run away unto them [joined them willingly].... And so they departed the 14ᵗʰ September having with them from the fishing fleet some 400 maryners and fishermen, many volunteers, many compelled."

Mainwarring then returned to continue his buccaneering career against the Spanish until he too was pardoned and once again took up his king's cause and began to again hunt pirates who raided English shipping. His renewed efforts took him back to Newfoundland in 1621 just as Calvert was establishing his Colony of Avalonia there.

The "Gaze." The highest point of land overlooking Ferryland harbour, it was used as a "lookout" by Easton and other pirates who made their headquarters there in the 1600s to watch for any Royal Navy ships which might be hunting them. (Photo: Prowse — 1895.)

He found his old pirate headquarters were occupied by the latest pirate "king," one John Nutt who had raised a pirate fleet of his own in Newfoundland made up of disgruntled sailors fleeing the press gangs of the Royal Navy. At Ferryland, Nutt and his pirates seemed to have been welcomed by Calvert's governor Wynn, and it was suspected that Nutt was given this refuge in exchange for part of his booty, payable to Lord Baltimore.

Nutt sailed to England the next year, where he was tricked into giving himself up in exchange for a pardon, but instead was thrown into prison. Baltimore interceded on his behalf and bought his freedom further arousing suspicions that he and Nutt were some kind of partners. Calvert sent Nutt off to Ireland, possibly to oversee his estates there but Nutt soon returned to his pirating ways until a few years later when he seemed to simply disappear.

Calvert himself had no sooner arrived in his Colony of Avalonia in 1627 when he had his own encounter with the pirates of Newfoundland. He had barely landed his family baggage when Ferryland was attacked by French privateers led by the infamous Marquis de la Rade. The Marquis paid Ferryland a vicious visit in the early summer. The French had been raiding the English fishing stations for the past year and as Calvert arrived they had just left one of the outports of his colony in Cape Broyle harbour just a few miles north of Ferryland.

Baltimore took his own ship and commandeered a Royal Navy man o' war and gave chase after de la Rade. He surprised the French pirate in a cove in Cape Broyle harbour "but the French let slip their cables and made to sea as fast as they could leaving behind them both the English ships and sixty-seven of their own crew which I made prisoners. We followed the chase so long as we saw any possibility of coming up with them but they were much better of sail and we were forced to give over."

After about 1630 pirate activity seemed to drop off in Newfoundland waters for thirty years or so until the Anglo-Dutch wars began in the mid 1660s. During these wars the Dutch raided both French and English settlements in America as well as in Newfoundland.

One of the most adventurous and successful of the Dutch pirates was Admiral de Ruyter. During the ten years of warfare de Ruyter led his fleet in raids that were swift and devastating. He sacked and burned both New York and

Quebec as well as many small settlements in Newfoundland. In 1665 he raided, sacked, and burned both Placentia and St. John's in Newfoundland.

Dutch Admiral de Ruyter. Was one of Holland's most accomplished seafarers whose successes against the English and the French in the Dutch Wars of the 1660s and 1670s made him a terror of the seas. De Ruyter was not above a little piracy himself and often sent his subordinate captains to raid anyone and anywhere at will. Ferryland was the recipient of one of his raids in 1673. (Photo: Prowse — 1895.)

In September of 1673 one of de Ruyter's captains, Nicholas Boes, on his way back to Holland after successfully having once again captured New York stopped into Newfoundland to do some damage to the English there. His target was Ferryland where he put into the harbour and quickly had it under his control. He then proceeded to sack, plunder and burn Lord Baltimore's colony to the ground, including Baltimore's old governor's house. The Kirkes who then occupied the colony as proprietors, and were said to be the most successful family of the colony at that time are also said to have suffered the most. Although pirate raids per say became a thing of the past in the late years of the seventeenth century they were replaced by the raids of privateers during the 1690s and first decade or so of the 1700s as France and England warred almost continuously in the waters around Newfoundland fighting for possession of the island.

CHAPTER IV

The "Kingdom of Kirke"

$\mathfrak{I}$n London, Calvert pressed King Charles to grant him a new American colony. For all the king's seeming discouragement of Lord Baltimore's efforts he did not appear to resist Calvert's request too strongly. Calvert outlined to him the area south of the Virginia colony that he thought he could profitably develop and Charles agreed to give him a grant to it. The area lay south of the James River and the Virginia colony and tracked south to the Roanoke River in what is today the state of North Carolina. However, the Virginia Company objected to Calvert having this area, coveting it for their own expansion.

Charles gave into the pressure from the powerful trading Company and Calvert described another area north of the Virginia colony in the Chesapeake Bay area. Charles, perhaps a little leery of antagonizing the Virginians once again procrastinated on a decision and Calvert spent the next couple of years pestering the king for the grant. During that time Calvert's health failed. It appears the long years of striving to establish his Colony of Avalonia had simply worn him out through all the personal tragedies, tribulations, confrontations, confabulations, and religious and political intrigues and petty prejudices. Before the Royal seals and signatures could be affixed to the documents of title to the grant, Sir George Calvert died on April 15, 1632 and he was buried at St. Dunstan's Church.

The effort to establish his Colony of Avalonia had not only worn Calvert's health out but also the wealth of his considerable estates in England and Ireland. His son Cecil claimed that he had spent almost 30,000 pounds in the effort and given the remains of his financial assets upon his death one can perhaps believe it. Calvert's will, made the day before his death doled out only some 2,400 pounds to his sons and daughters and some "kindred at Kiplie in the north" (Kiplin). This however, was probably not all the money he had in store as he willed his son Cecil to "pay and discharge all my debts" and appointed two lifelong friends to be "overseers and supervisors" of other money left in trust to be paid out to his younger sons when they reached the age of twenty-one.

His son Cecil inherited all his "lands, goods, and chattels of what nature whatsoever...either in England or Ireland or elsewhere." Cecil would take the bequeath seriously and would spend the rest of his life struggling to maintain claim to and develop the colonies his father had endeavoured to establish both in Newfoundland and in New England.

Back in Newfoundland, Baltimore's colony at Ferryland had not been completely abandoned when he had left it in the fall of 1629. About fifty of the settlers had remained behind there under Calvert's agent, one Mr. Hoyle, who according to one long-time settler at Ferryland "was afterwards carried away by one Ralph Morley." Following the mysterious disappearance of agent Hoyle, Cecil Calvert lost no time in appointing a new governor for his Colony of Avalonia, sending out one Captain William Hill in the same year that his father died and he inherited both the titles to his colonies and the title to his Barony as Second Lord Baltimore.

Hill and the isolated colonists persevered for some years despite the claims of some like Sir William Vaughan who claimed that Ferryland "was the coldest harbour of the land, where those furious winds and Icy Mountains (icebergs) doe play, and beate the greatest parte of the year." Under the administration of Lord Cecil Baltimore however, the Colony of Avalonia ceased to be a commercial venture and the settlement of Ferryland struggled on as more of a subsistence colony, yet it continued to survive. Cecil Calvert now concentrated his energies and resources into developing his newly acquired colony in New England and his neglect of Avalonia would come back to haunt him severely and expensively in later years.

In 1637 Charles I made another of his divine decisions and granted the whole of the Avalon Peninsula — indeed the whole island of Newfoundland — to one of his favourite Knights, Sir David Kirke. Charles made Kirke supreme Lord and Governor over all the territories of his island colony of Newfoundland.

The grant to Kirke was to have far-reaching and fatal ramifications for the king himself in later years, but it had more immediate effects on the Calvert's claims to their Colony of Avalonia. It was to be a source of constant and costly confrontation and litigation for the Calvert family for some thirty years.

Sir David Kirke was born at Dieppe in 1597 during a period when it was occupied by the English, the son of an English wine merchant who removed to England with the outbreak of the Thirty Years War and settled permanently in London. Kirke's father became a partner of Sir William Hamilton who was a chief investor in the Company of Merchant Adventurers and had backed Lord Baltimore's efforts to establish his colony in Newfoundland. Hamilton and his Company were interested in taking Nova Scotia (Acadia) from the French and making it an English colony.

In 1627 Hamilton and Kirke's father obtained a patent to Nova Scotia although it was left to their own resources and devices as to how they wrested it from the French who claimed it as Acadia. That year Kirke senior recruited his sons David, and his four younger brothers, Louis, Thomas, John and James (Jarvis), outfitted them with three men o' war and sent them off to take Nova Scotia. "Commodore" Kirke and his fleet captured the French stronghold of Port Royale and then went on to Quebec up the St. Lawrence River where they demanded the surrender of New France from its governor Samuel de Champlain.

The aging Father of New France defiantly refused their summons and the Kirkes sailed away. On their way through the Gulf of St. Lawrence they encountered a French fleet of four vessels on its way with relief supplies for Quebec and after a brief battle captured it.

Two years later Kirke led a larger fleet of six warships and three pinnaces against the French and sailed up the St. Lawrence River to Quebec City which this time Champlain did surrender being once again out of supplies in July of 1629. With his victory the English believed they had crushed the hopes of France to establish a New France in North America. While two of his brothers were left in Quebec to govern it, David returned to England.

Samuel de Champlain. Known as the "Father of New France" after his founding of the colony of Quebec in 1608, he was Governor of New France when Kirke captured New France for England in 1629. He was reappointed Governor when Quebec was handed back to France in 1632 by the Treaty of St. Germain-en-Laye. He died two years later from an illness at the age of sixty-five, worn out by more than thirty years of warfare with the Iroquois and the English. (Photo: Public Archives of Canada [MUN-CNS].)

Kirke has been described as "one of the most remarkable heroes of his age; his gallant capture of Quebec and destruction of French power in Canada, the most brilliant naval exploit in Canadian history." Others have described him as "a high-handed tyrant who disposed of his time equally between exacting harsh tributes from defenseless fishermen and debauching them with liquor."

On his return voyage to England after the capture of Quebec, Kirke stopped into Ferryland where he was acquainted with Baltimore's colony and had a first-hand look at the growing settlement with its impressive Governor's Mansion, well-built houses, its safe and busy harbour, and flourishing fishery. There can be no doubt that Kirke marked the place well on his maps and in his mind.

Upon arriving in England, Kirke was stunned to learn that the war between England and France had ended even as he had been fighting to capture Quebec and that Charles I had agreed by the treaty that had ended the war to return to France any possession that had been taken by the English after the treaty date.

The war had ended only a month after Kirke had set sail for America. All his efforts there had been in vain. The possessions cited in the treaty included all ports, ships, furs, fish, and other merchandise captured by his expedition in North America. In essence, Quebec and New France were handed back to the French and everything Kirke had captured was confiscated and he found himself unpaid for his efforts.

He thought he was being placated however, when the French said they were willing to award him 20,000 pounds in ransom for his prizes of ships, fur and fish — no doubt much less than their worth — not to mention the grand prize itself, Quebec and New France. But the French reneged on their promise once they had recovered their property and Kirke received nothing in payment for his adventure. Kirke could only have been outraged and embittered by this blatant betrayal. It probably hardened him to trusting in anyone or any means other than his own to ensure that his future endeavours would be rewarded financially.

He appealed to King Charles for some recompense for his efforts and the king appeased him by granting him a Knighthood in 1633 and four years later on November 13, 1637 giving him and three others a patent to the Colony of Newfoundland. He was made the first governor of the entire island and his grant patent was considered to supersede all others made before it, including Calvert's whom the king considered to have abandoned his claims there by virtue of his removing to New England.

The first colonial governor of Newfoundland went out to his domain in the spring of 1638 taking 100 colonists with him. He chose Ferryland as headquarters for his administration and promptly moved into Calvert's Manor House, expelling Baltimore's governor Hill and all his people claiming he needed the house for his wife and family: Lady Sarah Kirke and their three sons, George, David and Philip.

Kirke lost no time asserting his complete and absolute rule over the entire colony of Newfoundland. Knowing that the French once again held Canada, he realized that his colony was just as vulnerable to attack by them as theirs had been by him. He at once began to train his colonists as militia, and had gun batteries set up at Ferryland, Bay Bulls and St. John's harbours. He also got down to making his colony a paying proposition.

Kirke's partners in England, one of whom was the Duke of Hamilton, who together with Kirke's father had financed his expedition to Quebec ten years earlier, sent out large ships laden with cargoes of supplies and provisions for the fishermen which were to be exchanged for fish which was to be shipped directly to the Mediterranean markets cutting out the middlemen who were the West Country Merchants Company.

The Grant to the Duke of Hamilton & Sir David Kirke To the Island of Newfoundland: 13th November 1637.

The Rights to the Grant to Kirke were similar to those given to Calvert in 1621 but were inclusive of the "whole island", that is all the land "... being divided from the Continent by an arm of the sea ...".

The "Patent" was to "... Last 51 years. The Crown to have ten percent, thereof, and giving account of all gold etc., ... The Proprietors confirmed in all things but the fishing, and the sole trade of the country except the fishing. .... Power not to pay any tax.... Their ships not to be detained at any port except in case of invasion of England. Everyone over Twelve years old to take the oaths upon the Holy Evangelists before Hamilton, Kirke or his Deputy to establish the orthodox religion .... Power to transport necessaries tither ... All his subjects to aide and assist them."

IRONICALLY, IT WAS 51 YEARS TO THE DAY THAT FRANCE AND ENGLAND ONCE AGAIN WENT TO WAR IN 1688 AND LESS THAN TEN YEARS LATER THE KIRKE DYNASTY WAS ALL BUT WIPED OUT FROM THE FERRYLAND AREA.

Sir David Kirke's Grant to Newfoundland. Kirke and three other "adventurer-entrepreneurs," the Duke of Hamilton and the Earls Pembroke and Holland, were granted a patent to the whole Island of Newfoundland by Charles I in 1637. It was not a Proprietary Grant as was Calvert's in 1621 but Kirke and his partners treated it as such. Kirke laid claim to all of the island of Newfoundland and everything in it including Calvert's Colony of Avalonia. His abrogation of Calvert's property rights was to be the cause of no end of trouble for Cecil Calvert who had inherited the colony at Ferryland.

Kirke's enterprise showed immediate profit. He also expanded his business by trading to the West Indies – particularly for rum, and to the sack ships of the New England colonies from which he saw considerable profits. Soon, Ferryland was a popular entry port for the New Englanders and so began Kirke's lucrative but unpopular system of taxation.

He began to charge the seasonal fishermen from England for yearly leases on their rooms, and those who refused to pay were forced to leave the premises at cannon point. Those who refused to pay and were evicted complained loudly back home in London and Liverpool.

The governor also instituted another tax on foreign fishermen, which usually meant the French. He decreed that five fish of every 120 caught by a foreigner be paid as tax to his "Government." He sent out his armed ships to patrol the coves and bays of his domain and any who refused to pay the tax were threatened with the gun. When Kirke had arrived with his 100 settlers it was said that thirty of them were his manservants; in all likelihood they were his ship's crew who acted as his deputies and enforcers. Kirke was so dogged in collecting his foreigner tax that the French ambassador complained loudly in the halls of King Charles's court.

Kirke's Coat of Arms. The Coat of Arms issued to Kirke and his partners in 1638 is seen here in its original form as it was granted by the English "King" of Arms, Sir John Burroughs. The Coat of Arms was later cleaned up to the version we see today although it has gone through several subtle changes through the centuries. (Photo: *Part of the Main: An Illustrated History of Newfoundland and Labrador.* 1986. [MUN-CNS].)

In May of 1639 the French ambassador reported: "I have been informed that the said Kerq [Kirke] has a patent from the King of Great Britain to collect something on the cod fishery and that they propose to take this not only from British subjects but also from all those who go there to fish. This will be contrary to all justice and to the freedom which has been enjoyed there up to this time. I surmise that the King of Great Britain does not know what has been done and that no one but his subjects will submit to this."

Newfoundland and Labrador Coat of Arms. The "modern" version of the Coat of Arms granted to Kirke by King Charles I is today the offical Coat of Arms of the province of Newfoundland and Labrador.

Having just concluded a war with France, Charles decided to investigate the charges against Kirke and referred them to his Privy Council. They concluded that the Commission given to Kirke allowed him to tax the French "in justification." Charles was obliged to go along with Kirke's decrees and no action was taken against him.

In October of 1639, Kirke sent his own report to the king. In it we find traces of his staunch Royalist support and his firm belief that the king was the head of the Church of England. It reveals that he was definitely anti anything that did not agree with his Church. "Out of 100 persons brought over," Kirke wrote, "only one died of sickness. The air of Newfoundland agrees perfectly well with all God's creatures except Jesuits and Schismatics. A great mortality amongst the former tribe so affrighted my Lord Baltimore that he utterly deserted the country...of the other sect [Puritans] many frenzies are heard from their next neighbouring Plantation [Virginia] the greatest His Majesty hath in America. Their chiefest safety is in a strict observance of the rites and service of the Church of England."

Fervent Monarchist and Protestant, the sentiments Kirke expressed then would cause him much grief and distress only a decade or so later. His cavalier dismissal of Baltimore and his popists and veiled threats against the Puritans of Virginia seemed to confirm that he was somewhat religiously intolerant.

Not having been censured by the king, and knowing that he was well within his rights by the terms of his patent, Kirke pressed on with his schemes to make Avalonia a profitable venture. He did the unthinkable as far as the West Country Merchants were concerned — he offered to hire men to work in the fishery. In 1640 he offered wages to anyone who wanted to work in the shore fishery — to be byeboatmen, as they came to be called. Until Kirke's time all fishermen were members of the crews who sailed the ships out from England each year and were paid a share of the season's catch. Kirke offered to pay any man who would fish on his own and sell his catch to the governor.

For the West Country Merchants this was the final affront to their authority and greatest threat to their profits. They complained loudly and bitterly to King Charles but again no fault could be found with Kirke's actions. It took complaints by Kirke's own partners before his administration was held up to question.

Sir David Kirke. Soldier-Knight-Governor, Kirke was seen as a hero by some and as a pirate by others. He was considered a traitor by Frenchmen for his capture of Quebec and a tyrant by Englishmen who opposed his methods in Newfoundland. His governor-ship of Newfoundland was controversial from the outset. He showed little tolerance for any religion other than the Church of England and alienated the powerful West Country merchants by offering to hire men to work in the fishery and pay them wages. (Photo: B.F. — Newfoundland Museum [Hereinafter NM].)

The sins of Kirke continued to be counted against him by his adversaries. The goods he traded to the West Indies and Yankee sack ships were often paid for with cheap West Indian rum. Kirke decided to go into the liquor retail business and became what was probably Newfoundland's first Liquor Commission. He opened Newfoundland's first grog shop, operating it out of his Governor's Mansion. Fishing captains who had paid him for provisions with their rum now found themselves buying it back at Kirke's tavern at inflated prices.

Kirke set up grog shops in all the settlements of his domain from St. John's to Trepassey and beyond, and did a thriving business. He intimidated some of the local merchants into becoming his liquor agents, as one of them put it, "he enticed them to take licenses off him for ye selling of wine and other liquors and made them pay great rents yearly for the same and this Deponent take and pay for such a license 15 pounds per annum."

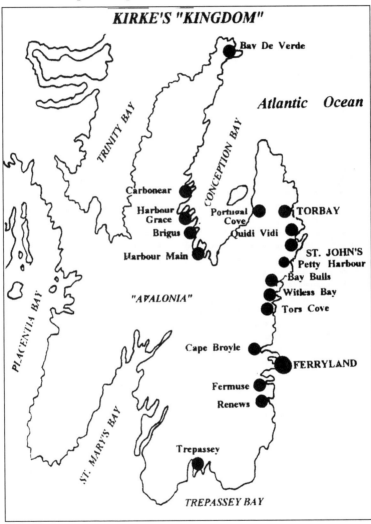

KIRKE'S "KINGDOM"

Bay De Verde

Atlantic Ocean

TRINITY BAY

CONCEPTION BAY

Carbonear

Harbour Grace

Portugal Cove

TORBAY

Brigus

Quidi Vidi

Harbour Main

ST. JOHN'S
Petty Harbour

"AVALONIA"

Bay Bulls

Witless Bay

Tors Cove

PLACENTIA BAY

Cape Broyle

FERRYLAND

Fermuse

Renews

ST. MARY'S BAY

Trepassey

TREPASSEY BAY

Map — Kirke's Kingdom. Kirke's kingdom encompassed eighteen major settlements and dozens of smaller outports all along the Avalon Peninsula from Bay de Verde in the northwest in Trinity Bay throughout Conception Bay and south along the "Shore" to Trepassey. (Map: B.F.)

This charge in the Puritanical age of England was totally opposed to the Puritan ethic of work without any smoking, drinking, or dancing. Kirke's grog shops, in the words of one of his coerced agents, resulted in him drawing and keeping "ship's masters, fishermen and others from their fishing employments to the great prejudice and hindrance of their voyages."

To many, Kirke's greatest sin was in his neglect to provide his wards with any places of worship. Despite his professions to the king that the Church of England was the only true one he apparently did little to foster it in Newfoundland. As one of his critics claimed: "There was not any Church, and if one should be built people would be too far away to come to Church through the woods."

Complaints like these had aroused the West Country Merchants into a near state of frenzy. But still King Charles would not act upon them until Kirke's own partners began to complain about his administration. It seems Kirke was not as forthcoming with their shares of the profits from the colony as he should have been. When his partners, Mssrs. Hamilton, Pembroke and Holland also began complaining about their governor's activities, King Charles decided to look into the accusations. In the minds of Kirke's partners it appeared to them that Kirke had adopted the old Scotsman's advice to his sons: "Make money honestly, if you can, but make money."

Kirke's partners decided to replace him with a new governor, whose authority was backed by the king. In June of 1640 Kirke's partners appointed John Downing their new executive officer in their colony and sent him to Ferryland with the instructions that: "In regard to Sir David Kirke he is to come over hither, we would have you to stay and remain in the house in Ferryland, wherein Sir David Kirke now dweleth, until you shall receive advice from us what to do."

Downing arrived late in the summer and found that Kirke had under his command "fifty-six guns, mounted in forts at Ferryland, St. John's and Bay Bulls...the forts fitted with small arms...and manned by the inhabitants." In his arrogant way, Kirke told Downing to stand aside and Downing saw that Kirke had the firepower to make him do so. Kirke wrote the king and Privy Council reminding them of the *Star Chamber Rules* which guaranteed his rights while at the same time vigorously denying the charges brought against him.

Kirke wrote: "...Before God all they have alleged against me is most false. Many of the fishermen this year, upon what grounds I know not, have driven in their stages and cookroomes much that ye most civil and wisest men amongst them did complain to me of these outrages.... I confess that he who would interrupt the fishing of Newfoundland which is one of the most considerable Businesses for the Kingdom of His Majesty and benefit of his Subjects and navigation is worthy the name of Traitor, the least thought and imagination where I do abhor..." He closes with the hope that by "good proofs" he will "clear himself from causeless clamours against him."

Kirke's influence with Charles must have been substantial. He carried on in Newfoundland despite the complaints against him. His real troubles began not in Newfoundland but at home in England when Charles began his tyrannical rule. A staunch Royalist, Kirke made no bones about where his loyalties lay when civil war broke out in England. King Charles now had more pressing problems to focus on right at home and little time for wayward governors in far-off colonies. At stake was keeping his crown as well as his head.

Civil War broke out in England in 1642 and Kirke's opponents there had more concerns at home than in the colony of Newfoundland. As the war went badly for the Monarchy many Royalists sought refuge outside the country and some of them saw Kirke's colony in Newfoundland as a safe haven. He had no popists or schismists residing there and his colony was well fortified.

The Duke of Hamilton. He was Kirke's father's partner in their venture to take Nova Scotia (Acadia) from the French in 1627. Ten years later Hamilton and the Earls Pembroke and Holland enlisted Kirke to be their governor in their new colony of Newfoundland after King Charles I considered that all other claims there like Baltimore's had been abandoned. (Photo: B.F. — Prowse — 1895.)

Through the war, Kirke flew the Royal standard of England above his Governor's Mansion in Ferryland and provided a refuge for many of the migratory fishermen who wanted to stay in Newfoundland because of their Royalist loyalties. Indeed, Kirke recruited fishermen to the Royalist cause. He offered them higher wages to work in the fishery, but it is believed he was actually enticing them into the ranks of his private navy.

At one point in the war Kirke offered King Charles sanctuary in his colony when it seemed he would lose to the Parliamentary Army of Oliver Cromwell. Charles should have accepted his offer.

While a prisoner of Cromwell on the Isle of Wight in 1648 however, Charles wrote Kirke asking him to provide refuge for his sister, fearing for her life and the lives of her family. This "sister" was one Lady Frances Hopkins who arrived in Kirke's colony with her family the following year. Another of the obscure characters in Ferryland's history, the king's reference to her as Kirke's sister only served to further obscure her identity. It is now believed that Charles was using the term "sister" in a royal connotation and that she was actually a sister-in-law of Kirke's, possibly even his wife's sister. She is now believed to have been the wife of one Sir William

Hopkins, host of the king while he was being held prisoner prior to his execution.

In any event, she pitched right in with the Kirkes once she arrived in Newfoundland and went on to become one of Ferryland's most successful planter families along with the Kirkes. It is not certain what happened to Sir William but he quite possibly suffered the same fate as the king given there is no record of him having arrived in the colony with Lady Frances and her family.

With the regicide of Charles I in 1649 the merchant factions who had so opposed Kirke's rule in Newfoundland now found new allies in the Parliament of the new Commonwealth of Cromwell. The next year they brought new charges against Kirke alleging that he had taken part in political activities hostile to the new Government, had shown favour to the French which was tantamount to treason, and was decidedly unfriendly towards the Commonwealth.

In 1650 the Long Parliament of Cromwell acted on the complaints of the West Country Merchants and this time Kirke had no recourse. Commissioners were sent out to take possession of Kirke's colony. They were authorized to "take possession of all arms, ammunition and fishing equipment belonging to Kirke." The Commission had with them one Captain Thomas Thoroughgood who was further authorized to arrest Kirke and take him back to England to face charges.

The case brought against Kirke dragged on in the Commonwealth Court for more than a year and Kirke was obliged to remain in England during the inquiry. In 1651 the Court ruled that: "Sir David Kirke had no authority in Newfoundland, and that all forts, stages, houses, and other appurtenances relating to the fishing trade and established on the island should be forfeited to the Government."

In spite of his Royalist sympathies, Kirke once again proved he was a survivor. He struck a deal with the Cromwellian

Puritans that saw him reinstated to his claims in Newfoundland, sans his "ordnance and other military equipment." It seems he gave up part of his grant to Cromwell's son-in-law, one Colonel Claypole, and subsequently was allowed to retain much of his property and claims in Newfoundland.

Some reports claim that Kirke languished in prison in London until his death in 1654, but others believe that he was allowed to return to Newfoundland where he resumed his residence as an ordinary planter. After striking his deal with Cromwell, instructions were given to the Commonwealth governor sent out to Newfoundland under the auspices of the interregnum, one Mr. Treworgie, to stay the seizing of Kirke's personal property and land holdings and allow him to reside in the colony.

Oliver Cromwell: Lord Protector of the Commonwealth. Cromwell overthrew the Monarchy in bloody civil wars in the 1640s. Ever fearful of the rise of Royalists who wanted to restore it, he had Kirke recalled from his post as Governor of Newfoundland and pressed charges against him. Knowing he was a confirmed Royalist, Cromwell seized the chance to "dethrone" Kirke and seize all his property in the colony. (Photo: B.F. — Prowse — 1895.)

Cromwell's governor Treworgie was installed in Baltimore's Manor Mansion and took possession of the adjacent land which had been part of Kirke's property but Kirke was allowed to keep his other land holdings in and around Ferryland. A descendant of Kirke's, Henry Kirke, wrote an account of Sir David Kirke's life about 200 years later in which he claimed that Sir David did return to Newfoundland and Ferryland and died there about two years later in 1654 at the age of fifty-six. He further claimed that Kirke was buried in Ferryland but to date no trace of his burial site has been found.

Kirke's widow, Lady Sara Kirke, carried on the legacy of her husband in the settlement of Ferryland, if not as the town's official head family, then at least as its most influential and prosperous one. When the Monarchy was restored in England in 1660 under King Charles II, eldest son of the beheaded Charles I, Lady Sara petitioned him to instate her eldest son George as governor of the colony his father had granted to her husband.

Charles II however, was not too anxious to repeat the mistakes of his father and become the second Charles to lose his head to the mindless mobs of London. He needed to know if it was the "people's will." Accordingly, Lady Sara had "certaine householders and inhabitants of Avalone" petition the king in 1666 to appoint her son George to the proprietorship of the colony. All her pleas and petitions fell on deaf ears. It was just not politically safe just then for Charles II to stir up the sleeping dogs of Royalists and Parliamentarians in England.

But not everyone was willing to let sleeping dogs lie. The Calverts were as dogged as ever about regaining their ownership to Avalonia as the Kirke's were in having theirs reinstated. After his return to England in 1630 and his application to King Charles I for a new grant in Virginia, Lord Baltimore was successful in his bid and was granted a tract of land in New England in 1632. Just before the paperwork was completed on the transaction however, Lord Baltimore died and his eldest son Cecil became heir to the new colony in America. Since then, Cecil Calvert, Lord Baltimore II, had been contesting the claims of Kirke to his father's Newfoundland colony. This may have been part of the reason why Charles II was reluctant to grant Lady Sara Kirke any kind of outright ownership to the property.

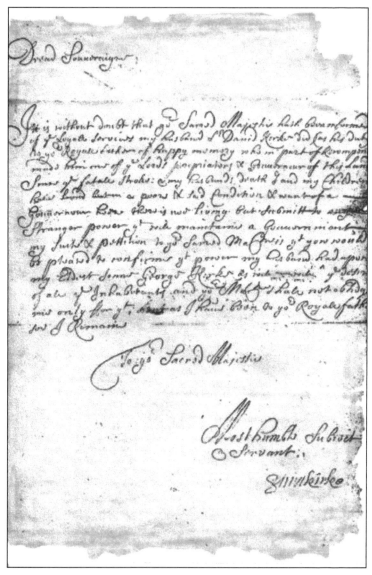

Lady Sara Kirke's Letter to King Charles II. In it she asked the king to give her eldest son George the same rights of ownership to the Colony of Newfoundland that his father Charles I had given to her husband in 1637. (Photo: MUN-CNS.)

Lady Sara Kirke's sworn supporters stated that: "...for 7 or 8 years before the arrival of Sir David Kirke, Baltimore never had possession or person there upon the property." Sir Cecil Calvert begged to differ.

Lord Baltimore II testified that Captain Hill, who had been left as Calvert's governor upon Baltimore's departure, "took possession and gave him [Cecil Calvert] a yearly account of his proceedings and the profit, and resided four or five years in Lord Baltimore's house in Ferryland...whereupon in 1638 Sir D. Kirke went to Ferryland in Newfoundland, and by force of arms turned Captain Hill out of Lord Baltimore's chief Mansion house (where the said Lord Baltimore had at the time divers things of good value) and took possession of the whole province and of divers cattle and horses belonging to Lord Baltimore."

Sir Cecil then prayed that through the redress of Parliament his father's property which had been seized by the Commonwealth Commissioners sent to dispossess Kirke, be returned to him. Sir Cecil also meant a reinstatement of the title to the Colony of Avalonia.

Sir David Kirke's administration as the first governor of England's first colony has been both criticized and applauded by history. By his contemporaries he was considered to be the absolute power in the colony who exacted from both friend and foe the same dues. He taxed the fishermen, auctioned off fishing rooms, confiscated salt and resold it at inflated prices, opened grog houses to resell the cheap rum he had bartered for at higher prices, forced fishing captains from their berths in order to give them to his friends, and totally neglected the spiritual well-being of his charges.

He so angered the West Country Merchants and their greedy enterprises that they appealed to the Commonwealth Parliament so vehemently that it finally decided to deal with this "notorious malignant." As a Royalist, Kirke was feared and charged with plotting against the Cromwellian Commonwealth.

Sir David Kirke's sins are seen by many as being too loyal and too royal. Some historians have painted him as either a tyrant or a martyr. His loyalty to the English Crown was well known and the refuge he afforded King Charles's sister resulted in her survival and her becoming along with Lady Kirke one of the more prosperous planters in Ferryland during the late 1600s.

Kirke has been lauded on one hand as "one of the most remarkable heroes of his age," whose service to his "pusillanimous" king was rewarded with "true Stuart ingratitude." Another characterizes him as an iron-fisted capitalist who was nothing more than a rum-runner and publican.

"There was a bar in every harbour," one critic claims, "and Kirke was importing rum and wine into Newfoundland in bulk; not by the 'barrel' but by the 'ship' full." Kirke was definitely an entrepreneur as his widow and sons showed for years after his death. Lady Sara died in 1680 but her sons continued their Ferryland plantation until 1696 when the French destroyed Ferryland and carried the Kirke's sons off into captivity. Kirke's contest with the Calvert's over valid ownership of Avalonia continued for years and was never really resolved during the years of the Cromwell Protectorate. Kirke died a broken man but not a destroyed one.

Whatever Kirke's reasons for wanting to establish a solid colony at Ferryland, he was the first to set up a successful government in Newfoundland, albeit a somewhat financially biased one towards himself. He was the first to contest the monopoly of the West Country Merchants and show that the colony could sustain itself given the chance, that it was fit for year-round habitation, and could be more than merely "a great English ship moored near the Grand Banks for the fishing season for the convenience of fishermen." He was also first to recognize and point out the significance and importance of Newfoundland as a sentinel to the Gulf of St.

Lawrence and the gateway to the heart of New France at Quebec. This insight was to prove prophetic in the next century as England and France engaged in a century of conflict that did not end until the defeat of Napoleon at Waterloo in 1815.

In the words of the Newfoundland historian D.W. Prowse: "...the old West Countrymen swore their testimony against him as boldly, as uniformly, and unblushingly as a corporal's guard in a brush with civilians. No doubt Sir David was a tyrant, a bold, determined ruler who kept everybody in order.... In excuse for him it should be remembered that he had no salary..."

Perhaps Kirke's real legacy in Newfoundland is loyalty and liquor.

PROFILE — Avalonia and Maryland: The Baltimore Connection

Lord Baltimore's petition to King Charles in 1629 for a new grant to land in the Virginia colonies was not received too well by His Highness. Charles's initial reaction was to suggest that Calvert give up any further notions of colonization in America. Calvert was persistent and with support from what few friends he had left in the Royal court and Parliament he lobbied the king for two years. But these were hard years for the Lord who was barely fifty years old. Personal grief and the stresses of trying to fulfill his dreams of colonization must have taken a heavy toll on him both physically and mentally. He spent most of the next two or so years in London as he sought his grant but also made frequent trips to his estate in Wexford, Ireland.

Calvert's application for a grant in New England was almost a carbon copy of the one he had received for Avalonia. In his request for the patent, he once again asked for rights as a *Palatinate*, the feudal seigneury of the medieval type. The grant would give him rights second only to the king and make him absolute Lord over his colony with complete control over its administration, defense, and the upkeep of his plantation. All writs were to run in his name, in the name of the king. The Charter also contained a clause that stipulated every interpretation of its terms should always be "beneficial, profitable, and favourable" to the patentee.

The land Calvert had set his eyes on to colonize in New England was in the Chesapeake Bay area north of the

Virginia colony and its Puritan settlers. This may have been a slight factor in Charles's granting the patent to Baltimore. It was the Puritans who sought grants in America to pursue religious freedom, and it was the Puritan Parliament of Oliver Cromwell to whom Charles would lose his head a couple of decades later.

Map — The New England Colonies, 1633. *Terra Mariae* or Mary's Land, as Calvert requested it be named after King Charles I's wife Queen Henrietta Mary, was a sprawling tract of land in Chesapeake Bay that covered some 12,000,000 acres. The Charter for Maryland as it would later be called, was unique among the patents given to Companies that established the other New England colonies. Maryland became the seventh colony of the original thirteen colonies to join together as the United States in 1738. Baltimore, named for its founder, was established on the banks of the Patapsco River under the rule of Charles Calvert, fifth Lord Baltimore. (Map: B.F.)

After the first area he proposed was turned down because of opposition from the Virginia Company he proposed a second area in the Chesapeake Bay area north of them. It lay on the Potomac river and stretched north to the 40th latitude, east to the Atlantic Ocean and west to the headwaters of the river on what is today the southern border of Pennsylvania. In all it comprised about 12,000,000 acres of virgin territory. The land had been originally granted to the Virginia Company, but they had done nothing to develop it and the king considered himself free to dispose of it because the Virginia Company's Charter had been annulled in 1624.

Ironically, one of those who opposed Calvert in his New England bid was Sir William Vaughan, his original bene-factor who had sold him land to start up his Colony of Avalonia. In 1630, the year Calvert returned to England, Vaughan wrote his treatise on colonization of America, the *Newlander's Cure*. In it he wrote of Calvert's attempt to estab-lish his Newfoundland colony.

"The disaster which happened to my Lord Baltimore," he wrote, "and his colony last winter at Ferryland in our New-land Plantation, by reason of scurvy, have moved me to insert some more specific remedies against that disease...." After giving some recipes for anti-scurvy concoctions he goes on to berate and give detailed reasons why Baltimore's attempt failed. "...Before the said Lord ever began his Plantation, he cannot deny but I advised him to erect his habitations in the bottom of the bay at Aquaforte, two leagues distant from that place [Ferryland] which for ought I hear is not much to be commended, and more into the land where my people had wintered two years before and found no such inconvenience. Nay, his Lordship himself suspected the place; for in his letters he complained that unless he might be beholding to me for the assignment of both of these places out of my grant, he was in a manner disheartened to plant on that coast by reason of the easterly winds; which with the mountains of ice floating from *Estotiland* [Iceland] and other northern coun-tries towards Newfoundland render that shore exceedingly cold. Yet notwithstanding; his Lordship being persuaded by some which had more experience in the gainful trade of the fishery than in the situation of a commodious seat for the wintering of his new inhabitants, bestowed all his charge of building at Ferryland, the coldest harbour of the land where most furious winds and icy mountains do play and beat the greatest part of the year. Whereas if he had built at Aquaforte or in the westerly part of the Bay of Placentia, which hath above fifty miles overland betwixt it and that eastern shore, his enterprise would have succeeded most luckily, and to this of Ferryland might have served well for his profit in the fishing and also for a pleasant summer dwelling.

"Sir Francis Tanfield, under the Right Honourable the Lord Viscount Falkland, continued two years but three leagues more southward at Renews, and did well enough, in which place likewise my colony remained one winter without any such mortal accidents."

Icebergs like this one were a common sight along the shore of Ferryland harbour in Baltimore's time just as they are today. Even Calvert's promoter, Sir William Vaughan, complained that Calvert quit his colony because he was "disheartened to plant on that coast by reason of the easterly winds; which with the mountains of ice floating from Estotiland [Iceland] and other northern countries towards Newfoundland render that shore exceedingly cold." (Photo: Courtesy K. Mooney. *Southern Scenics*.)

Vaughan's evaluation of Calvert's "failed" Ferryland can be taken at face value. Unlike Lord Baltimore, he had never visited his colony in the "Golden Island" and never experienced those "furious winds and icy mountains" he so eloquently described in absentia.

Despite even Vaughan's criticisms, Calvert was successful in securing his new grant from Charles I. In giving Calvert his patent in New England, the king cited the fact that he had done so because the region was uninhabited and possessed only by "Barbarians, Heathens, and Savages."

By early 1632, Calvert knew that his patent had been granted but before the seals could be affixed to the documents Sir George Calvert died on April 15, 1632. The name of his eldest son Cecil Calvert, was inserted on the documents and deeds to the Mary's Land colony and he inherited his father's dream as well as his headaches. It now became Lord Cecil's job to make the plantation of Mary's Land a reality. From the outset, Lord Baltimore II found out exactly what his father had had to endure. Opposition to the Mary's Land plantation was immediate and loud in the king's court from the Virginia Company interests. To protect his own, Cecil enlisted the aid of his younger brother Leonard to act as his governor of the new colony.

Due to the obstacles and opposition placed in his way, it took Sir Cecil nearly a year and a half to organize an expedition to the colony. On November 22, 1633 two ships, the *Ark* and the *Dove* under command of Cecil's brother and Governor Leonard, and manned by 200 men set sail from Cowes on the Isle of Wight to brave the wilderness of America where they would encounter the aboriginals of the New World.

While Sir Cecil contended with the administrative headaches of dealing with the Virginia Company and the Puritan religious bigots in England, his brother Leonard as governor adopted a fair but firm policy in dealing with the native peoples of the colony. The governor's treatment of the Indians he encountered resulted in a harmony that was in marked contrast to that of the colonists of Virginia and other New England colonies.

Lord Baltimore II also succeeded in establishing a religious tolerance in the colony brought about largely by his granting the colonists increasing legislative powers. In spite of all the obstacles, interference, and opposition, the Colony of Maryland as it soon came to be called, continued to grow and prosper over the next several years.

But Sir Cecil experienced almost as soon as his father had, the toll the responsibility and financial burden could take on a man. He had married Anne Arundell, the daughter of the wealthy Baron Arundell of Wardour who had been a close friend of his father and had convinced Sir George to convert to Catholicism. Cecil had gained some property and wealth from both his marriage and his father's estate, but within six years he was forced to liquidate it to support his colony in Maryland.

His father-in-law wrote a close friend in 1638 that: "My son Baltimore [Cecil] is brought so low with his setting forward the plantation of Maryland, and with the clamorous suits and oppositions which he hath met withall in that business, as that I doe not see how he would subsist if I doe not give him dyett, for himself, his wife, his children and servants."

Sir Cecil however, like his father persevered and continued to administer the Colony of Maryland from England for forty-two years until his death in 1675. Unlike his father, he never set foot in the colony he had founded and administered for over forty years. But the Colony of Maryland pressed on under a successive ruling clan of Calvert-Baltimores.

When Sir Cecil died his title fell to is son Charles, Lord Baltimore III. Charles Calvert went out to the colony at the age of twenty-four and remained there as its governor until his father's death when he returned to England. When he arrived home he found that his own son, Leonard, named for his uncle who had been Maryland's first governor, had renounced his Catholic faith and as a reward had been elected to Parliament. Charles disowned his son but when Charles died in 1715 his Protestant son inherited the title of Lord Baltimore III and also became Governor of Maryland. He held the title and the position for only two months when he suddenly died. The title of Lord Baltimore fell to his 16-year-old son Charles who did not visit Maryland until 22 years later in 1737.

From the founding of Maryland in 1632 until the outbreak of the American Revolution in 1775, the reins of power in the colony remained firmly in the hands of the Calverts as the Barons of Baltimore and the Lords Proprietary of the Maryland plantation. Title and rule fell to successive generations of the Calvert family and the governor was also always a Calvert by birth or an in-law by marriage. The last Proprietary of the colony fell to Henry Harford, the illegitimate son of the sixth and last "belted" Baron of Baltimore, Frederick Calvert. The last governor of the colony was Robert Eden, who was Frederick's brother-in-law by virtue of having married his sister Caroline. By 1775 however, all had become a moot point. The colonials of America had had enough of their British overseers. The concept of owning fiefdoms or plantations or colonies was no longer acceptable to Americans. The American Revolution cemented the point.

Much has been said about Sir George Calvert's contribution to the colonization of America, both in Newfoundland and Maryland. Like all true pioneers he has been described as every variant between a saint and a sinner. In most cases it depended on which side of the cross he was picked to be crucified on.

The Calvert Family Coat of Arms. The Calvert Coat of Arms was probably granted around the time Sir George was knighted in 1617. With his Arms Calvert chose as supporters a pair of leopards. After his death his son Cecil modified the Arms after he established the Colony of Maryland to include elements of his grandmother's family, the Croslands, adding a cross that was commemorative of one of her ancestors who had fought in the Crusades, placing her family back to the mid-1300s. Cecil also adapted the Arms to become the Seal of Maryland, replacing the leopard supporters with the figures of a fisherman and a "planter," or farmer, to represent both the colonies of Maryland in America and Avalonia in Newfoundland. The Motto reads: "*Fatti Maschi Parole Femine,*" an old Italian proverb meaning "Deeds are for Men—Words are for Women." The Escutcheon, or Shield of the Arms, is today incorporated into the Seal and Crest of the State of Maryland, unique in the United States as they come from a colonial era. (Photo: MUN-CNS.)

"On one side," wrote D.W. Prowse, "he is lauded as a saint, whilst some extreme writers have denounced him as a bigot. With his bastard son (reportedly his second son Leonard Calvert) he can hardly be called a saint, but he was far ahead of his time in enlightenment; his religion was real and sincere; his zeal for the Catholic faith was genuine and honest; it was opposed to all his worldly interests...he was neither an epoch maker nor an empire founder, simply an honest religious Cavalier."

A later President of the United States, James Buchanan, said of Calvert: "In an age of religious bigotry and intolerance Lord Baltimore was the first legislator who proclaimed the right of conscience, and established for the government of his colony the principle not merely of toleration, but perfect religious freedom and equality among all sects of Christians. He was in advance of his age, but he became the precursor of a principle which is destined in the end to prevail throughout Christendom..."

BARONS OF BALTIMORE
And
LORDS PROPRIETARY OF MARYLAND

Calvert Proprietors of Maryland

1632 — Cecil Calvert: Second Lord Baltimore
1675 — Charles Calvert: Third Lord Baltimore
1715 — Benedict Calvert: Fourth Lord Baltimore
1715 — Charles Calvert: Fifth Lord Baltimore
1751 — Frederick Calvert: Sixth Lord Baltimore
1771 — Henry Harford: (Son of Frederick)

Calvert Governors of Maryland

Leonard Calvert: 1633
Philip Calvert: 1660
Charles Calvert: 1661
William Calvert: 1670
Cecil Calvert: 1676
Benedict Calvert: 1684
Charles Calvert: 1697
Charles Calvert: 1720
Benedict Leonard Calvert: 1727
Charles Calvert: 1732
Robert Eden: 1768

Baltimore is today the largest city of the state of Maryland. But it was not the founding settlement of the colony of "Mary's Land." The founding settlement was St. Mary's City in Chesapeake Bay but it was later moved to Annapolis farther inland due to troubles with the Puritan Virginians.

THE BARONS BALTIMORE

LORD BALTIMORE II
Cecil Calvert - 1632

LORD BALTIMORE III
Charles Calvert - 1675

LORD BALTIMORE IV
Benedict Calvert - 1715

LORD BALTIMORE V
Charles Calvert - 1715

LORD BALTIMORE VI
Frederick Calvert - 1751

(Photos: Enoch Pratt Free Library, Baltimore, Maryland.)

CHAPTER V

The French Invade... And The Dutch Raid

$\mathfrak{F}$erryland was not a very tranquil place during the regime of the English Commonwealth throughout the 1650s. Tensions, suspicions, and prejudices permeated the place. The Lord Protector of the Commonwealth, Oliver Cromwell, decided that the Colony of Newfoundland should have a proper government "for managing and ordering the affairs and interests of this Commonwealth in Newfoundland." To guard against the irregularities indulged in by other appointed Governors with the vested interests of their patentees or themselves in mind, Commissioners of the Council of the Commonwealth were appointed, and unlike a single Governor who held absolute authority, the Commissioners had to have a majority vote among them to enact or carry out any decisions they might make.

In 1652 four Commissioners were sent out to the island and their instructions upon arrival were quite clear. The first thing they were to do was ensure that no one but themselves had control of any guns there. "...Upon your arrival there, you...shall take into your hands and possessions and keep for the use of the Commonwealth...all the ordnance, and ammunition...." The new Commonwealth was still nervous about the Royalist movement and any bids it might make to restore the Monarchy. They were instructed "to use your utmost endeavour to secure the fishery there against Rupert [Prince Rupert who was actively engaged in the cause of restoring the Monarchy] or any others that shall attempt to disturb or interrupt it..."

The second thing they were to do was to take control of the commerce of the colony. After they had all the guns under their control they were to take control of the fishery by confiscating unto their own administration all "...houses, boats, stages and other appurtenances belonging to the fishing trade being in Ferryland or in any other place in Newfoundland."

This last instruction was aimed particularly at Sir David Kirke as the Commonwealth sought to dispossess him and confiscate for the Commonwealth what it felt was due it. The powers that were considered that Kirke owed the state back taxes, so to speak. "...Considerable sums of money," the Commissioners were informed, were to be forfeited to the Commonwealth, "and are alleged to be in the hands of Sir David Kirke and others.... You are to use all care and diligence in the examination and discovering of what is due to the Commonwealth from Sir David Kirke and others...and upon discovery thereof you are to take care...in such manner as may be most for the service and advantage of the Commonwealth."

While Kirke and his family were permitted to retain some holdings in Ferryland and continue as common planters they had lost all their status and were carefully watched to see that they could not regain any of their former station and power. The Kirkes had another problem as well as the Commonwealth. The Calverts still claimed ownership of the Colony of Avalonia and therefore anything the Kirkes might have been allowed to retain by the Commonwealth.

Cecil Calvert, Lord Baltimore's son, spent the entire decade in court in litigation with the Kirkes and the Commonwealth trying to retain the ownership he felt rightfully belonged to the Calvert estate. Dozens of depositions were sent back and forth across the Atlantic with sworn statements from supporters on both sides of the argument. The Council of the Commonwealth was none too eager to settle the matter in either's favour. Both sides, as far as they were concerned, were belted aristocracy draped with the trappings of Baronies and Knighthoods that still reeked with the Royal stench of the Monarchy.

Just what the Commonwealth period of England meant for the common planter and fisherman of Avalonia and the other colonies of Newfoundland has been long debated. Some see the period as a repressive one where the regime conducted the affairs of the colony of Newfoundland as an almost social if not outright communist state. Others, such as Prowse, believe that the Commonwealth period was one in which "the settlement, trade, and fisheries of the Colony were largely increased; no injustice to planters was permitted under [its] firm control; the cultivation of the land was encouraged; trade between the island and the continental colonies was promoted.... New England prospered immensely under the Commonwealth, and so did our island Colony. By the end of the Commonwealth period the New England trade was firmly established in our Colony."

Whether the Commonwealth was good for Newfoundland or not, its life span as a political regime was probably not long enough to have confirmed its worth or detriment. By 1660 the English had had enough of it and clamoured for a return to the Monarchy. It returned in the person of Charles II, eldest son of the dethroned Charles I. Young Charles had been living in exile in France since the troubles in England and was at once reluctant to reestablish close ties with former staunch Royalists for fear that he become the second Charles in a row to lose his head to English politics.

King Charles II. He took the throne when the monarchy was restored in England in 1660. Son of the beheaded Charles I he had lived the past twenty years of his life in exile in France under the protection of Louis XIV where he had married Louis's niece. He returned to England as a weak vassal of the French king and before leaving France had struck a deal with Louis that would allow the French to establish a colony on the island of Newfoundland at Placentia, literally the "backdoor" of Baltimore's colony at Ferryland. The deal was to have grave consequences for the settlers of Ferryland for almost fifty years to come as France and England waged war in Newfoundland for possession of the island. (Photo: *Wikipedia*.)

In France he had married the niece of the French king Louis XIV and this royal alliance was to be the cause of great concern as well as suffering for the colonists of Ferryland, and indeed for all the English settlers of Newfoundland for years to come. By the time Charles was restored to the throne he and Louis had formed an uneasy alliance which Charles's subjects eventually grew to rue and curse their sovereign for his perfidy. In 1662 Charles II gave Louis XIV permission to establish a colony on the shores of Newfoundland.

The French chose a site in Placentia Bay which was almost directly west of the settlement of Ferryland and which the English considered to be part of their Colony of Avalonia. The French called their colony Plaisance, which was later

Anglicized to Placentia which the bay and community are still named today.

By 1665 the French had established a substantial settlement at Placentia with housing for about 100 French and Basque fishermen and their families, and a garrison of some thirty Regular French Army soldiers. They had also erected a fort and outer batteries mounting 18 cannons. "By this betrayal of English territory and English rights Charles planted in our midst our most bitter rival; he exposed our infant settlements to those murderous raids afterwards made on the English planters." So wrote Prowse concerning the secret treaty made between England and France during their uneasy alliance in their war with Holland. In all likelihood it was probably a concession Charles made to Louis in exchange for his support against the powerful Dutch who were contesting England's colonies in America and the East Indies.

By virtue of the pact, Charles handed over to Louis possession of almost the entire island of Newfoundland, from Cape Race on the southern tip of the Avalon Peninsula west to Cape Ray at Port aux Basques, north around the Great Northern peninsula and south and east to Cape Bonavista. It was virtually all of the island save for Trinity and Conception Bays and the east coast of the Avalon Peninsula which came to be called the Shore. The area ceded to the French would become known as the French Shore and much of it would remain so for 250 years.

The English planters on the island had no idea that the pact had been struck until the French actually took up residence at *Plaisance*. On a summer's morning in 1662, one Issac Dethick, the sole English planter at Placentia, was surprised to see "a great French ship full of men and women put into Grand Placentia, where she landed a great number of soldiers and passengers who fortified the harbour with 18 pieces of ordnance...." Dethick saw "...the Governor's Commission under the Great Seal of France for the command of the whole country of Newfoundland" and was unceremoniously expelled from the premises.

Map — The Robinson Map, 1669. A detail of this map shows the "French Trading to and from Placentia Bay" which was being used by the French to supply their colony at Placentia which they had established with the "sufferance" of Charles II. (Photo: MUN-CNS.)

The French were firmly entrenched by late that year when news of their arrival reached Ferryland. Even then it came only by happenstance. By 1662 Sir Cecil Calvert had reaffirmed his title to his father's grant to Avalonia after his long contest with the Kirkes, and had appointed two governors to administer his colony. The Governor, one Captain Pearce, and his Lieutenant, one Mr. Raynor, hired sheriffs to collect the fishing room rents and to generally look out to the order of the colony.

Calvert's governors at Ferryland had been receiving complaints about a Mr. Russell who harboured at St. Mary's Bay in the southwest corner of the Baltimore plantation, and facts that he was behind in his room rent and was engaging in over hunting and trapping with "Canadian Indians" who had been sent over by the French from New Brunswick and Nova Scotia and were wintering on the islands of St. Pierre and Miquelon off the island's south coast. Baltimore's governors sent out their deputy, one John Matthews, to arrest Russell and the chief of the Indians.

Matthews reported: "In the yeare 1662...I was sent by...the right Honble. Governors with their warrants to St. Mary's Bay to bring one Mr. Russell, ye inhabitant there, and ye master of ye Indians...before them to Ferryland; but instead of having the warrant obeyed, a French Captain seized on me demanding what I came for. I replyed for ye said Mr. Russell and ye master of ye Indians to go before ye Governors to answer and give an account of their actions for making an attempt upon ye Islande without any authority from His Majesty of Great Brittaine; which he scornfully answered, saying we had no power there nor in any other of ye Southern parts of ye Lande but all did belong to ye French Kinge whereupon I averring that our King was King thereof and of all for about 30 or 40 leagues around about it, was taken prisoner and so kept for about two days when ye French carried me aboard and sett forward until we came nigh *Plaisance* Fort which was furnished with 28 guns from whence a shallop came out from ye Governor with command for our return to St. Mary's in pursuit of ye Indians where by God's providence I made my escape."

Matthew's encounter was reported to England by Lady Hopkins, who personally complained to her nephew Charles II about the French presence in their English colony. "The island has been without a Governor [until 1661]," she wrote, "and the French taking notice thereof have settled a garrison...which in Sir David Kirke's time they never dirst [dared] attempt.... The Governor of ye French keeps ten vessels all ye winter there which carry 30 or 40 men apiece and are very well suited to coast [sail]...sufficient to destroy the Plantation [Ferryland]..." Evidently even close family friends were kept out of Charles's secret plans and he was unwilling to confirm or even respond to the fact that he had made a pact with the French.

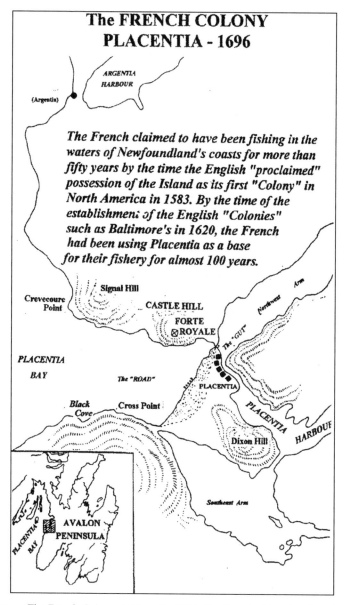

The FRENCH COLONY
PLACENTIA - 1696

ARGENTIA
HARBOUR

(Argentia)

The French claimed to have been fishing in the waters of Newfoundland's coasts for more than fifty years by the time the English "proclaimed" possession of the Island as its first "Colony" in North America in 1583. By the time of the establishment of the English "Colonies" such as Baltimore's in 1620, the French had been using Placentia as a base for their fishery for almost 100 years.

Signal Hill

Crevecoure
Point

CASTLE HILL

FORTE
⊗ROYALE

Northwest
Arm

The "GUT"

PLACENTIA
BAY

The "ROAD"

PLACENTIA

Black
Cove

Cross Point

PLACENTIA HARBOUR

Dixon Hill

PLACENTIA BAY

AVALON
PENINSULA

Southeast Arm

Map — The French Colony at Placentia 1696. The French claimed to have been fishing in the waters of Newfoundland as long or longer than the English. During the war with the Dutch in the 1660s, as an ally of the English, Louis XIV succeeded in gaining a Grant from Charles II to most of what France later claimed to be their territory in Newfoundland. (Map: B.F.)

King Louis XIV of France. Louis became king in 1643 and determined to have his share of the riches of America. Known as the Sun King because of the splendour of his reign he also called himself the most Christian King of Europe, an obvious slight to his lifelong adversaries, the Protestant Kings of England. He made a secret pact with Charles II of England to surreptitiously rule that kingdom and things went well until Charles died and his Catholic brother James II was forced to flee England and the throne was taken over by his inveterate enemy, the Protestant William of Orange of Holland. From 1689 until his death in 1715, Louis was almost constantly at war both on the continent of Europe and in America. Those wars caused much suffering for both French and English settlers and fishermen in Newfoundland. (Photo: B.F. - NMM.)

The fears of the Ferryland settlers were allayed somewhat when both England and France joined forces in a war against Holland. For a brief time, the English settlers of Newfoundland had no reason to fear raids by French privateers. The Dutch however, who also had claims in America, did prowl the coastal waters of the island harassing fishing ships and other vessels of both countries for the next decade as the English, French, and Dutch engaged in a series of wars. During that time the Dutch made no concerted attacks on any of the settlements but that was to change in 1673.

That year, the king of Holland, William of Orange, sent a fleet under that country's most famous and accomplished admiral, de Ruyter, to New England to reclaim what the Dutch had originally established there as New Amsterdam, or New Holland. De Ruyter sacked New York and nearby settlements and carried off most of the colony's settlers, including the governor of New York, Dudley Lovelace. On their return to

Holland, de Ruyter detached a contingent of warships to raid the English settlements along Newfoundland's coast in an effort to inflict even greater damage on the English colonies in America. One of their targets was to be Ferryland and the Colony of Avalonia.

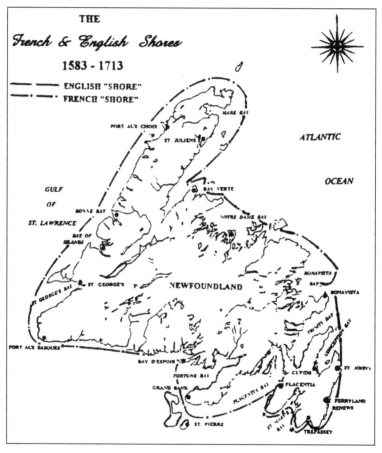

Map — The French Shore, 1583–1713. The French Shore was claimed by France all around the coast of Newfoundland from Cape Bonavista on the northeast coast up the Northern peninsula and south down the west coast of the island and east again to Placentia on the western boundary of Baltimore's Colony of Avalonia. The English had traditionally fished from Cape Bonavista to Trepassey along the coast of the Avalon Peninsula and did not venture much into the waters along the south coast of the island. The Treaty of Utrecht of 1713 saw the French having to give up most of its claim to these areas. (Map: B.F.)

It is believed Ferryland was singled out because the Dutch thought it was the capital of the colony since it had the governor's seat of office positioned there. Four Dutch warships: the *Green Wife*, 40 guns; the *Arms of Leyden*, 40 guns; the *Schacator*, 36 guns; and the *Unity*, 36 guns, under command of Admiral Nicholas de Boes sailed into Ferryland Harbour on September 4, 1673. Governor Lovelace of New York recorded a detailed account of the event.

The Dutch ships entered the harbour unopposed, he recorded, and although the place was fortified with "four great guns, the fort being out of repair, and no commander upon the place," the settlers offered no resistance. De Boes and his men then systematically "plundered, ruined, fired, and destroyed the commodities, cattle, household goods, and other stores belonging to these inhabitants...." He gave a list of fourteen of the settlers who suffered losses "and many others to the value of 2,000 pounds." Included among the "fired and destroyed" items was the Baltimore-Kirke Mansion which the Dutch took particular pains to destroy.

Dutch Warships. Three Dutch warships like the ones pictured here attacked Ferryland in the summer of 1673 sacking and destroying the settlement and carrying off most of its settlers and fishermen into captivity. (Photo: Bowen: *The Sea: Its History and Romance to 1697.* MUN-CNS.)

At that time lady Kirke was still in Ferryland with her extended family: son George and his wife with four children, David and wife with one child, and Philip who was still unmarried. She also had 66 manservants in her employ with 14 boats, three stages, and three oil vats. Whether the Dutch knew who she was or merely singled her out because of her prosperity, Lovelace considered that: "Lady Kirke and her family were the greatest sufferers on this occasion."

The next day with the settlement in near complete ruin, the Dutch began to destroy the colony's means of livelihood. They confiscated all the fish in the harbour and burned thirty fishing boats then demanded that the settlers deliver up to each of the four ships six hogs and one bullock in exchange for them sparing them some little shelter and food for the coming winter. With the Colony of Avalonia in ruins and the abandoned settlers nearly completely destitute, the Dutch sailed on to a small fishing village about three miles to the north on September 9 where they found one Mr. William Pollard, apparently a quite prosperous fisherman-merchant.

They "plundered him of 400 quintals of fish, provisions, and household stuff amounting to 400 pounds sterling. They likewise burned at that place 40 fishing boats, the house, warehouses, etc. belonging to the fishery in that harbour, besides several English prizes [ships and their cargoes] which they brought to their general rendezvous at Fayal [the Azores]."

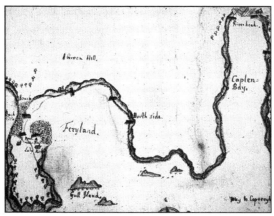

Map — James Yonge Map 1663. This map clearly shows the location of the Kirke's "Pool" plantation identifying one of the houses as "Lady Kirke." (Photo: MUN-CNS.)

Later that year both England and France sued for peace with Holland and the hapless settlers of the Newfoundland colonies were left to their own devices to rebuild their lives. The irony of the Dutch destruction of Ferryland is that the defenses set up by Kirke forty years earlier and dismantled by the Commonwealth Government could have prevented the plunder. The Dutch Admiral de Boes later commented that if the harbour of Ferryland had been defended by cannon "he would not have ventured in."

The Colony of Avalonia recovered and rebuilt and began to prosper once again over the next decade or so when once again events in far-off Europe took their convoluted turn and spread their far reaching effects to the colonies in the New World. In 1685 Charles II died and his brother James succeeded to the throne. James II was a confirmed Catholic and had even convinced his brother to convert to that faith on his death bed. Again the ugly head of religious bigotry reared its contorted face in England and within three years James II was forced to flee the country for his life when his Protestant brother-in-law, Prince William of Orange of Holland, eagerly accepted the invitation of the English to sit on their throne and champion their cause.

King James II of England. He took the throne as a Catholic after the death of Charles II but had to flee England for his life when the people rebelled against his efforts to restore Catholicism as the state religion of England. With the help of Louis of France, he attempted to regain the crown, but his forces were defeated in Ireland at the Battle of the Boyne by William of Orange in July 1690. James again fled to France where he spent the rest of his life in exile. (Photo: *Wikipedia.*)

With William's ascent of the English throne, King Louis of France became the implacable enemy of the English Crown.

Louis hated William the Protestant Dutchman as much as the Protestant Dutchman hated Louis the Catholic Frenchman. By now Louis had regained control of New France and had a firm foothold on the island of Newfoundland at his fortress colony of Placentia. By 1688 England and France were at war. In Newfoundland the "kingdom of Kirke" was at an end and Baltimore's dream of an Avalonia was a mere mist. But the settlers of Ferryland who had stubbornly carried on there were about to enter the most punishing era of their existence.

In 1689 Louis moved first to vanquish the English in America. The newly appointed governor of New France, Compte de Frontenac, arrived in Quebec and immediately sent a three-pronged attack against the New England colonies. He also sent troops to reinforce the colony at Placentia and garrison the island of St. Pierre off the island's south coast. The settlers at Ferryland became alarmed at the French buildup just 70 miles or so to the west of them and appealed to the home Government for protection.

The home Government had more pressing problems in New England to contend with and delayed any response to its colony of Newfoundland. Once again, the settlers of Ferryland were left on their own, and once again showed the resourcefulness to act on their own.

During 1688-89 the war had not yet come to the shores of Newfoundland but was well underway for the fishermen on the high seas whose vessels were being constantly raided by French ships. The French governor of Placentia, Sieur de Parat, went so far to try to convince the English that no state of war existed that he invited some of the leading merchants of St. John's and Ferryland to visit him at his colony in Placentia.

French and English Warships. At the beginning of the "nine Years War" of 1689–1697 both French and English raided each other's fishing vessels in the coastal waters off Newfoundland. (Photo: Leslie *Life Aboard a British Privateer.* 1894. MUN-CNS.)

There, Parat showed the Englishmen his fortifications, the prosperity of his colony, lavished them with the best of his food larder and wine cellar, and told tales of his colony's wealth. It was to prove a grave mistake. The English saw just what poor shape his colony was really in and decided to attack it before it attacked them.

On February 25, 1690 forty-five English buccaneers crossed the seventy miles overland from Ferryland to attack Placentia. They were led by Herman Williamson, one of the Englishmen Parat had so lavishly entertained at his governor's house a few months earlier.

In the early morning hours, the buccaneers had no trouble entering the sleeping town, surprising the dozing sentries, killing two of them and wounding the Lieutenant of the Guard, one Mon. de Costabelle, with a musket ball in his back. It was a bad shot: Costabelle would return some time later to exact his revenge.

Within minutes the English had captured all the fortifications and seized all of the buildings in the town. Governor Parat was dragged from his bed and hauled up before his captors. He immediately recognized Williamson as one of his guests from the previous fall. Williamson demanded the wealth Parat had bragged about and the governor told him he did not have any.

Not believing him, Williamson had Parat tied to a chair and slivers of wood poked under his toenails and lit afire. To ensure the governor would talk, a second fire was lit in a pot and placed under his chair. The besieged and unlucky Parat did not remain silent long. Williamson found that the governor's bragging had been just that. The French colony was even poorer than the English settlements on the island.

Frustrated, Williamson's privateers took the only two ships in the harbour and loaded them with all the valuables they could find in the settlement. They dumped the fort's cannons into the sea, tore down the walls of the forts, destroyed all the belongings, arms, furniture, fishing boats and other supplies they could find, and otherwise left the place in a complete shambles before withdrawing to Ferryland in their captured prize ships, after holding the French colony in a grip of terror for six weeks. Parat later reported: "After the attack, the inhabitants found themselves in the same state as if they had been shipwrecked on a deserted coast."

William of Orange. The Dutch Protestant Prince was "invited" by the English to take the throne of England in 1689 after they had dethroned the Catholic James II. William was married to James's Protestant daughter Mary who ruled jointly with him. William was an implacable enemy of Catholics, particularly Louis XIV of France and lost no time in starting a "nine Years War" with France that lasted from 1689 to 1697. In Newfoundland that war was to be the cause of much grief and hardship for the settlers of Ferryland as several times the colony was sacked and destroyed by the French from their colony at Placentia. (Photo: *Wikipedia*.)

The French presence in Newfoundland had been dealt a severe blow by the privateers of Ferryland who were in fear of their own security, and it took the French several years to recover from the attack. But once they did they retaliated with a fury.

Feeling an advantage, the English decided to press it. In 1692 they sent a fleet of five men-o'-war against Placentia, determined to destroy the French presence on the island. To their surprise they found the fortifications there to be rebuilt and they could not enter the harbour under the guns of the new forts and batteries.

In the time since the English attack from Ferryland, a new governor, Jacques Francoise de Brouillon, had arrived to take charge and had immediately undertook to better defend the settlement and its approaches from the sea. De Brouillon was a "gentleman" and an ex-infantry officer who upon his arrival had found the colony in the "shambles" the English had left it and the garrison there consisting of only seventeen soldiers under command of the recovering de Costabelle. He had made fortifying the colony his first priority.

He had brought with him some veterans of the French military, one of them being a gallant and cavalier young Engineer of the French Army, the Baron de la Hontan. He set de la Hontan to work planning and building the new defenses of the colony. By 1694 the French had decided they would take complete control of the fishery in Newfoundland and oust the English settlers from the island. In North America the war with the British was going all in their favour and they decided to hold the island of Newfoundland as the guardian to the Gulf of St. Lawrence and their stronghold of Quebec in the heart of New France.

Placentia's new governor spent the winter of 1693-94 planning an expedition to destroy the English settlements on the Avalon Peninsula, and Ferryland was to be his first target.

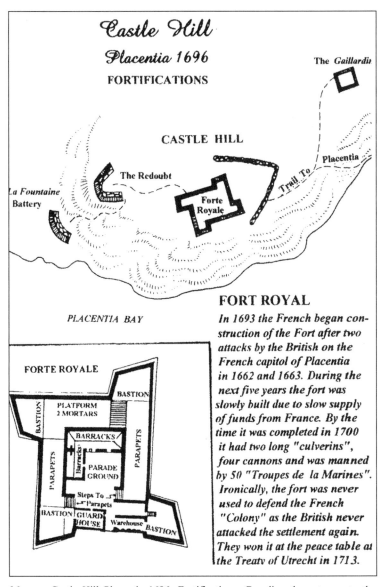

Castle Hill

Placentia 1696

FORTIFICATIONS

The *Gaillardis*

CASTLE HILL

Placentia

The Redoubt

Trail To

La Fountaine Battery

Forte Royale

FORT ROYAL

PLACENTIA BAY

FORTE ROYALE

BASTION

PLATFORM 2 MORTARS

BARRACKS

BASTION

Barracks

PARAPETS

PARADE GROUND

PARAPETS

Steps To Parapets

BASTION GUARD HOUSE

Warehouse

BASTION

In 1693 the French began construction of the Fort after two attacks by the British on the French capitol of Placentia in 1662 and 1663. During the next five years the fort was slowly built due to slow supply of funds from France. By the time it was completed in 1700 it had two long "culverins", four cannons and was manned by 50 "Troupes de la Marines". Ironically, the fort was never used to defend the French "Colony" as the British never attacked the settlement again. They won it at the peace table at the Treaty of Utrecht in 1713.

Map — Castle Hill Placentia 1696: Fortifications. Guarding the entrance to the French colony of Placentia, it was fortified with the large and impregnable Forte Royale that sat atop the hill as well as three outer batteries that overlooked the approaches to the settlement below. (Map: B.F.)

PROFILE — Placentia: The French In Newfoundland

In 1662 the French were allowed by the English king Charles II to establish a colony on the island of Newfoundland. They chose a site in Placentia Bay and named it *Plaisance*, and the bay and community that survive there today are called by their English name, Placentia. The French had been using Placentia Bay and the harbour of the same name there as a kind of fishing capital of their Newfoundland fishery for over 100 years according to their claims, before they established their colony there.

The site of their colony was almost due west of Ferryland, the main settlement of Lord Baltimore's Colony of Avalonia, and occupied the western portion of his grant. When Baltimore's officials went there to investigate the French presence on the site they were told they were trespassing on French territory and unceremoniously expelled under threats of imprisonment.

Between 1662 and the outbreak of war between France and England in 1689, the French colony at Placentia was raided four times by English privateers from Newfoundland and on several occasions by Yankee privateers from the New England colonies. Shortly after a raid by Ferryland privateers in 1690, the French realized that Placentia was important to their plans to wrest Newfoundland and the New England colonies from the British.

By 1692 they had sent a military governor to fortify the colony, which move proved to be a sound one as the Placentia colony proved to be a tactical thorn in the side of the British in their wars with the French in North America. Newfoundland and its settlements were to suffer severe hardships over a period of almost 100 years during the long conflict between the two countries for possession of the continent. Lord Baltimore's chief settlement of his Colony of Avalonia, Ferryland, was one settlement that saw much devastation during the century of conflict between the two powers.

Since the voyage of John Cabot in 1497 the English had considered Newfoundland their discovery and by 1583 their possession by right of Sir Humphrey Gilbert's claim. The French claimed that Basques, Bretons, and Channel Islanders from France had been whaling and fishing in the waters of Terre Neuve for more than twenty years before Cabot's voyage.

The English coveted the rich fishing grounds of Newfoundland's Grand Banks and jealously hoarded them. Despite English protests in French Royal courts the French continued to fish in what they considered to be their traditional waters around the coasts of Newfoundland. The English had concentrated their fishing mainly in the waters on the east coast of the island from Cape Ray in the south to Cape Bonavista in the north. Even in the south around Trepassey Bay the French considered the English to be trespassing dangerously close to their fishing territory and thus the name of that bay.

To back their claim, the French recorded that as early as 1560 there were about 6,000 Basques in 200 ships fishing and whaling in the waters around Newfoundland. As well there were as many as 4,000 French in 120 ships fishing for cod from Notre Dame Bay in the north, all the way around the Northern Peninsula, south along the west coast and east along the south coast to St. Mary's Bay.

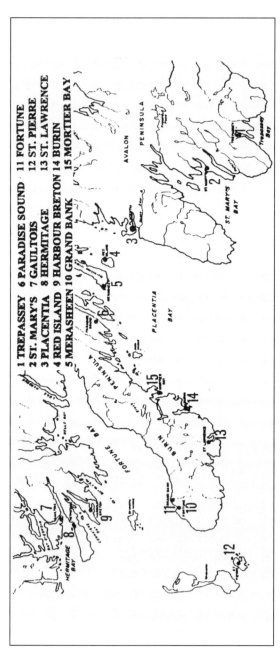

Map — The French Settlements in Newfoundland-1660. The French believed their claim to Newfoundland was as valid by virtue of the voyages of Jacques Cartier as the English claims were by the voyages of John Cabot and Humphrey Gilbert. By 1660 they had established yearly fishing stations along the south coast of Newfoundland from the islands of St. Pierre and Miquelon to Trepassey in St. Mary's Bay. English fishermen found in that Bay were called trespassers by the French and thus the name of the bay. After the official English claim to the island in 1583, the French considered only the coast of the Avalon Peninsula and north to Bonavista to be English "territory." By the mid 1600s the French claimed to have 15 permanent fishing stations on the island stretched along the south coast from Trepassey Bay to Heritage Bay. The trespassing of the English into those waters led to punitive raids by the French against the English fishery, one of which was Baltimore's colony at Ferryland. The most devastating was the raid by the Marquis de la Rade in 1628 and was one of the reasons Baltimore gave for quiting his colony in Newfoundland. (Map: B.F.)

The English, who were confident of their claim to Newfoundland, were outraged when the French were allowed to establish a colony at Placentia in 1662. The French-English wars throughout the eighteenth century saw several changes in both countries claims in Newfoundland and peace treaties often redefined the outcome of military victories.

Placentia was not the only place on the island to have permanent French settlements. Others, as the names suggest, were considered to be St. Mary's, Merasheen, Red Island, Paradise Sound, Mortier Bay, Burin, St. Lawrence, Fortune, Grand Bank, Hermitage, Gaultois and Harbour Breton. These settlements were sparsely scattered and populated, rarely numbering more than three or four families, but they were distinctly French. Even an English census in 1687 recorded that permanent French residents on the island numbered nearly 700 souls.

The Newfoundland fishery was as important to France as it was to England. After the Treaty of Utrecht in 1713 the French fought to retain concurrent fishing rights with the English in Newfoundland waters and won them. But they wanted exclusive rights in certain areas, particularly along the coasts of the Northern Peninsula and along the island's west coast in the Gulf of St. Lawrence.

After 1713, many Acadians were uprooted from Nova Scotia and looking to live independently sought to establish themselves on the French Shore along Newfoundland's west coast. Between 1713 and 1755 as many as 400 of them settled from the Codroy Valley to St. George's Bay, and even farther north into the Bay of Islands and Bonne Bay on the west coast of the island. Many others went on to Labrador where the French had been fishing and whaling for 150 years and established small fishing villages along its south coast, many of which survive today from Blanc Sablon to West St. Modeste.

In 1763 the French Shore was redefined and its limits moved north to Cape St. John on the Baie Verte Peninsula and south to Cape Ray on the southwest coast at Port aux Basques. It was an admission by the English that a French presence had existed on the west coast of Newfoundland, but not one that would interfere with their fishing enterprise on the east and northeast coasts.

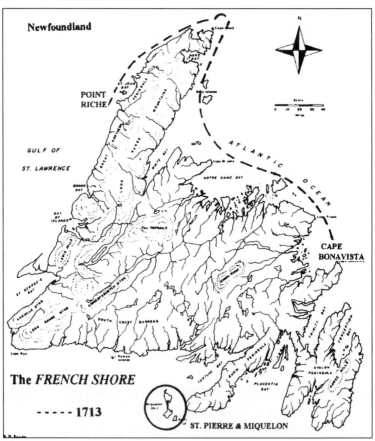

Map — The French Shore 1713. After the Treaty of Utrecht in 1713 and the expulsion of the French from Newfoundland, the limits of the French Shore were changed to run from Cape Bonavista and west around the Northern Peninsula and as far south only to Pointe Riche. The French had to give up their rights to fishing all along the south coast and most of the west coast of the island of Newfoundland. (Map: B.F.)

Plan of the Properties at Placentia 1713. The French properties at Placentia at the time of the British takeover in 1713. (Photo: PAC.)

By 1870 some estimates put the French population on the island of Newfoundland at 20,000 but this number was found to be a great exaggeration in 1874 by an official British census. That census recorded that there were about 9,000 people of French extraction living along the French Shore. It also showed that there were only three English settlements along that same shore.

While the English had basically ignored the French Shore, the displaced Acadians had established a brisk trade with Nova Scotia, Quebec and St. Pierre. Sandy Point in St. George's Bay was the unofficial capital and a thriving trade centre of the west coast of Newfoundland. Today there is a revitalized interest in the French culture brought to the area by the dispossessed Acadians of the 1700s, particularly in the Port au Port Peninsula area of the region and the French culture continues to survive and even flourish in certain parts of Newfoundland.

CHAPTER VI

Winter of the Tomahawk

Ferryland during the summer of 1696 was having a very successful fishing season. Seven or eight fishing ships had made the harbour their headquarters for the summer and the harbour was under the charge of one Captain William Holman whose ship the *William and Mary* was armed with 16 guns. It was about mid-August when he learned of the French plans to attack the English settlements along the Shore and that Ferryland was to be their first target. This news came to him from a couple of English fishermen who had been taken captive by the French somewhere along the shore earlier that summer and had managed to escape Placentia and make their way overland back to Ferryland.

When Holman heard the news he immediately went into action. He landed the cannon from his ship along with the fourteen guns the other ships carried and set them up in a series of four small, flimsy forts which he hastily constructed at strategic places on high ground along the shores of Ferryland harbour. He'd barely finished these hurried preparations on August 31 when de Brouillon's French fleet appeared around Ferryland Head out on the Downs. He saw that he faced a considerable force: seven French ships including five frigates of war, a bomb ketch and a fire-ship.

When the Ferryland fishermen saw the number of French ships most of them grabbed their muskets and gunny sacks and began to head inland to the woods. They believed they would have no chance against the greatly superior French force. Holman angrily threatened that if any man did not stay to defend the harbour he would confiscate that man's season's catch of cod and distribute it among those who stayed. He also threatened to burn their property, including their fishing premises and houses saving the French the trouble. Most of them believed him and returned to man the forts.

As the French ships closed Holman began a furious cannon fire upon them and kept up a five hour duel with the ships which could not manoeuver in the face of the concerted English fire. Holman's tiny forts held up and the French ship's suffered heavy damage during the long exchange of cannon balls. It was later learned that the French suffered eighty to ninety men killed in the battle.

In mid-October Commander Charles Desborow and a Royal Navy squadron arrived in Ferryland as Holman and the settlers were putting the settlement back together. Desborow reported to the Admiralty on Holman's able leadership and courageous defense of Ferryland. "Holman's greatest difficulty," Desborow wrote, "was to keep the inhabitants to his assistance...they did return and with his [Holman's] bravery and prudent management, they so battered the French men of war that they ran off...leaving their anchors and cables behind them and ye French lost eighty or ninety men..."

Holman's defense of Ferryland so impressed the Admiralty that they believed "it had so discouraged the French that they gave over their intended spoile, which might have ruined the whole country there being no more men of war to defend it." The Admiralty rewarded Holman's gallantry by awarding him with a "medal and gold chayne." Holman submitted an expense account to the Admiralty for his costs which came to a total of 495 pounds, a considerable amount even considering the damage done to the settlement. Most of it was found to be legitimate however, as the 150 pounds for spoiled fish to compensate the fishermen who lost their flakes and stages to the French cannon fire. He was compensated 345 pounds – the other 150 was disallowed but he did receive reimbursement of 12 pounds for the last item on his list which read: "1 hogshead of sherry wine and 20 gallons of brandy and a barrel of strong beer, which I gave the men to encourage them in time of fight."

Holman's Defense of Ferryland. Artist's depiction of the 'Defense of Ferryland' shows Holman's fort atop the hill battering the French ships below during their attack on Ferryland in the summer of 1694. Painting by Stewart Montgomerie. (Photo: Courtesy of Michelle O'Connell, The Colony Cafe, Ferryland.)

De Brouillon's failure to take Ferryland and other English settlements in 1694 so frustrated Governor Frontenac that he devised a new plan to capture the island of Newfoundland. In late summer of 1696 he informed Placentia that he was sending New France's foremost soldier-son, Pierre le Moyne Sieur d'Iberville, to help capture and destroy the English settlements. D'Iberville's campaign on the Avalon Peninsula was to be the first furious round in the long and savage bout between England and France for possession of North America.

D'Iberville left Quebec early in September with a force of 120 French-Canadian irregulars and *coureur de bois*, and picked up about eighty or ninety Abnaki and Micmac Indians in Acadia on his way through the Gulf of St. Lawrence. These men were hardened, tough, experienced Indian fighters having spent years on the Canadian-American frontier in wars with the Iroquois. When he arrived in Placentia later that month he found Governor de Brouillon had started without him. He had gone on without the French Canadian in the selfish hope that he could capture the English settlements alone and claim all the booty for himself.

Pierre le Moyne Sieur d'Iberville. Premier "soldier-son" of New France, D'Iberville was sent to Newfoundland to ravage the English fishery on the island and destroy the English settlements there during the winter of 1696–97. His efforts were very successful — he destroyed virtually every English settlement on the Avalon Peninsula and caused a devastation to the fishery that took the English years to recover from. (Photo: Mun-CNS.)

De Brouillon had been frustrated from the start. The prize he sought most, St. John's was too well defended for him to be able to enter the harbour so he turned south and captured the small harbour at Bay Bulls. The few fishermen there escaped into the woods along with Captain Thomas Cleasby and the crew of a Royal Navy ship, HMS *Sapphire*, and headed to Ferryland which Cleasby hoped to fortify and defend. Cleasby even denied the French the prize of a Royal Navy ship by scuttling the vessel and sending it to the bottom of the harbour before he retreated to Ferryland.

When the French arrived at Ferryland on September 21, Governor de Brouillon was in a foul mood and determined to have some conquest and prize for his effort. Captain Cleasby had arrived in the settlement only a day or so ahead of him and unlike two years earlier when Holman had defended the place found that there was nothing there now to make a fight of it with. Any fortifications and guns that had been in the harbour had been destroyed or carried off by the Dutch over twenty years earlier and none had been sent to the settlement to replace them. Cleasby had very little to fight with and the French reported that de Brouillon "carried Forillon {Ferryland] sword in hand, in spite of the vigorous resistance of Sieur Clasby [Cleasby], Captain of the *Zephyr* [*Sapphire*], who was made prisoner with all his men."

A Ferryland planter, John Clappe gave his own account of the French raid. "On Monday the 21st day of September [1696] seven sail of French ships of war and two fire ships landed about seven hundred men in Ferryland and attacked us on every side and after what resistance we could make against them (they being too many in number and too strong for us) we were forced to submit. And, for as much as we...refused to take an oath of fidelity to the French king and take up arms against your most gracious Majesty, the said enemy dealt very hardly with us, and burnt all our houses, household goods, fish, oil, train vats, stages, boats, nets, and all our fishing craft to the value of twelve thousand pounds sterling...and sent us away with our wives, children and servants, which are in number about 150 persons..."

The French looting included besides the burning of the town and about 30 fishing boats, prisoners de Brouillon hoped to ransom. The 150 Ferryland settlers were sent off to England where they spent the winter at Barnstaple and

Appledore in West Country Dorset. Captain Cleasby and the three Kirke brothers, George, Philip and David Jr. along with his wife Mary, were taken prisoner to Placentia. For all his rapid raiding up and down the coast of the Avalon Peninsula, Governor de Brouillon had little to show for his efforts when he sailed back into Placentia harbour in early October.

D'Iberville was not surprised by the governor's lack of success. He had been sent to conduct a land campaign against the English since it was already evident that places like St. John's could not be captured by sea attacks if those settlements were expecting and prepared for them.

The governor and the soldier argued about tactics and then about the division of the spoils and after several days wrangling came to an agreement on both. Plunder would be divided equally and de Brouillon would go by sea while d'Iberville would go by land. One force would support the other in their attacks.

On November 1, 1696, d'Iberville set out on his trek for Ferryland where he was to join up with de Brouillon's forces who left by ship. It is not clear if de Brouillon even informed d'Iberville that he had already sacked and destroyed Ferryland and if he had why d'Iberville insisted on making the journey there overland. He might just as well have gone in de Brouillon's ships. De Brouillon had left the smaller settlements of Renews and Fermews to be captured in his next sweep where he was directly headed now, but there was nothing to be dealt with between Placentia and Renews since Ferryland had already been destroyed and emptied of settlers. Given the animosity between the two it is quite possible that de Brouillon had not informed d'Iberville. What makes it even more perplexing is the gruelling trek d'Iberville experienced from Placentia to Ferryland to reach an empty and destroyed settlement.

French-Canadian Troops who fought the winter campaigns against the English in Newfoundland were more like the *coureur-de-bois* of Quebec than regular soldiers, hardened veterans of years of Indian fighting on the frontiers of America. (Photo: Parks Canada. Castle Hill Nat'l Hist. Park.)

For nine days d'Iberville's force slogged across the frozen countryside, through dense forests, over rock strewn hills, soft soggy bogs, around large ponds, across swift flowing rivers and streams, through knee-high snow drifts, and travelling the last two days of the trek short of food only to arrive and find all was in vain.

D'Iberville's chaplain, Abbe Jean Baudoin, who was on the expedition described the punishing trek. "On All Souls Day [November 1, 1696], we clambered about a league into the woods. The next day we trooped through a moist country, covered with moss, in which one could sink up to the middle of one's leg, often slipping on the ice, the weather already being very cold, especially in the mornings. We have walked nine days, sometimes in woods so thick that you could hardly get through, sometimes in a mossy country by rivers and lakes, often enough up to your belt in water. The 10th we arrived at Ferryland.... The way here could easily be done in five days in good weather. It would almost have been just as short to go to St. John's right away. We were beginning to lack victuals after two days. We found a dozen horses quite hit the spot, which did us for victuals until we had the *Profond*" [One of de Brouillon's ships which by then was in Renews].

After a couple days' rest, d'Iberville went by boat to Renews where he confronted de Brouillon about his wild goose chase to Ferryland. In the heated discussion that followed d'Iberville learned that the Placentia governor was jealous of the French-Canadian's authority and resented Frontenac sending him out to spoil his own victories. D'Iberville was miffed about his own situation and the two sides lined up in a heated encounter that came to drawn swords. One of de Brouillon's officers offered to run the French-Canadian through with his blade and a couple of d'Iberville's men offered to do the same to the governor. Both men had brought their chaplains with them on the expedition and the pair of clergymen got together to simmer the hotheads down and soon the cooler heads prevailed.

The Frenchmen spent the next several days clearing out the settlements in the coves between Renews and Caplin Bay [Calvert] and when their work was done had gathered up some 130 fishermen and planters as prisoners and confiscated 18 boats and 9,000 quintals of salt fish. While the prisoners were being transported by boat to one of the French ships for transport to England one of them, "...an Englishwoman threw herself into the sea and drowned." She was the only casualty of the otherwise bloodless victory of the French.

From Ferryland d'Iberville and de Brouillon agreed to part company and make their own ways towards St. John's. "God be praised," d'Iberville's chaplain Badouin recorded. "We all drink from the same glass." D'Iberville went on to plunder and destroy every English settlement on the Avalon Peninsula that coming winter, and all except the settlers of Carbonear in Conception Bay escaped being taken prisoners and deported. They had forted themselves up on Carbonear Island and successfully defended themselves against the French attack.

The winter became known to the English planters and fishermen as the "winter of the tomahawk." By the spring of 1697 the English Shore was all but devoid of population. Those who had escaped capture and deportation were dying of starvation and exposure to the winter in the woods surrounding their burned-out settlements.

A British military expedition under Colonel John Gibson sent out to repossess the island in the spring of 1697 reported on the state of the colony. Gibson wrote: "...nothing escaped the barbarous fury of the enemy.... To the southward of this, [St. John's where he landed] there was not an inhabitant left but two or three in the Bay of Bulls [Bay Bulls] and two at Brigus by South [Brigus South] and from that to Trepassey, which is the southmost of the English plantations, there is not a living soul left, yea not at Ferryland, which was always looked upon, as I am told, to be the best harbour and the pleasantest place in the whole Island. However, I intend whenever we have secured this harbour, to go to Ferryland with part of my regiment to secure that also, which possibly may encourage the people to come and settle there again and there are several other places to the southward of that, which in my humble opinion ought to be secured, and I am afraid if we do not the enemy will...before next spring, if a happy peace do not prevent it."

And a happy peace did prevent it. In September, England and France signed the Treaty of Ryswick and the nine years of hostilities called King William's War ended. The winter of 1696-97 was the only season since the Colony of Avalonia had been founded in 1621 that the settlement of Ferryland was not occupied by settlers. Those who had been deported to England spent the winter preparing to go back if they could get the support and protection they would need to carry on there. From their refuge in Barnstaple and Appledore in West Dorset, the displaced settlers of Ferryland petitioned the king for their return to their colony.

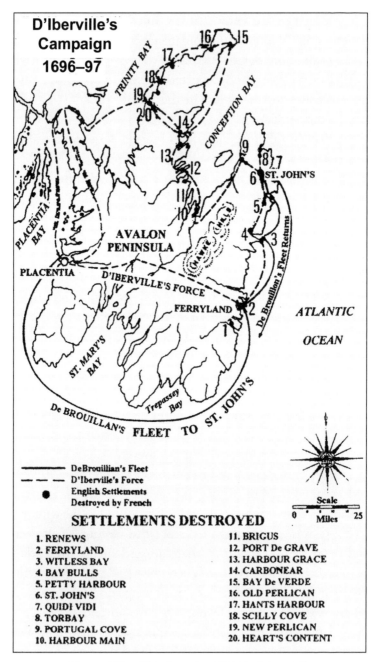

Map — D'Iberville's Campaign 1696–97. (Map: B.F.)

"We therefore humbly implore your most sacred Majesty," they petitioned King William, "for relief and that a sufficient number of frigates [warships] and land forces may be timely sent, that this next season for fishing may not be lost and to regain and defend the said harbour and other be possessed of our places for rebuilding our houses and stages and rooms for carrying on our fishing trade without any hinderance [sic.] or molestation..."

For those of Ferryland who had not been deported but carried off to Placentia as prisoners they were released late in the fall or early winter of 1697 and most were sent to St. John's, including Captain Cleasby and his ship's officers and the only surviving Kirke brother, George. His two brothers David Jr. and Philip had died during their short captivity in the prison at Placentia and George's health was suffering badly when he was released. With him went the widow of his brother David, Mary Kirke. The two surviving Kirkes did not return to Ferryland and George died soon after his release. Mary Kirke remained in St. John's for several years where she began a plantation there. Her failure to return to Ferryland immediately would be the cause of much hardship for her several years later when she tried to return there to claim the Kirke property of the Pool plantation.

By 1698 most of Ferrylands settlers had returned and for a short time enjoyed a precarious peace. But the plight of the colonists of Avalonia was just beginning. It would be almost another twenty years before they would see a lasting peace. Although they had petitioned the king to fortify their colony against future attacks their pleas appeared to have fallen on deaf ears. What they didn't know was that along with the Treaty Charles II had made with France in 1662 he had also made an agreement with the West Country Merchants in 1675 to provide "that the prosecution of the plantations in Newfoundland be discontinued."

Twenty years before the d'Iberville raid, King Charles II had issued a new charter to the merchant company undoing all previous grants. The charter had severe effects on the settlers of Avalonia as it did in all areas of the Newfoundland colony. It provided for the removal of all settlers from the island or if they chose to stay placed severe restrictions on them. They had to move inland six miles from the coastline so as not to compete with the fishermen of the West Country Merchants Company for the best fishing berths or rooms when they arrived in the spring. If they built habitations they would not be allowed to have chimneys, and no military protection would be provided.

This may have been one of the reasons why the French felt they could attack the English settlements with impunity. But the local merchants and planters fought back and refused to be removed despite the efforts of both the French and their own countrymen and Government. The "winter of the tomahawk" lasted for over a decade for the settlements of Avalonia.

During the winter of 1704-05 the French made another attempt to drive the English from Newfoundland. After another unsuccessful attack on St. John's they once again turned their attention to the Shore. They easily captured and laid waste to all the settlements from Petty Harbour to Ferryland where they encountered their first resistance. At first the colonists there showed signs of fight but as the main French force showed up they realized they had little chance against their superior numbers and raised the white flag. Their surrender did not spare them. The frustrated French governor of Placentia, St. Ovide, who had not been able to take St. John's after a prolonged siege, took his anger out on the settlement and once again burned it to the ground after pillaging it of everything of value. Again most of the settlers were shipped back to England, but many who had been fore-warned had escaped into the woods from where they gradually returned after the French departed. It was the third time in about thirty years that Baltimore's colony had been razed to the ground but still the settlers persisted.

Again the inhabitants of Ferryland appealed to the home Government to properly fortify their settlement. They argued that unless a fort was built in the town or a warship sent to protect them during the fishing season they would likely be ruined by the raids of the French. They defined their precarious situation and reminded Queen Anne how important the Ferryland fishery was to England and how much it had suffered in recent years.

Until the latest French attack, they reminded Her Majesty, "...forty of fifty ships were fishing out of Ferryland and nearby outports to the great advantage of Her Majesty's revenue, and bringing up thereby a numerous company of seamen for the Queen's service to the great benefit of the country..."

They also detailed how the fishery from Ferryland had drastically declined in recent years: "For in Ferryland and the adjoining harbours, Caplin Bay, Cape Broyle, Aquaforte, Fermuse, Renews, there hath been kept 86 boats by inhabitants and now, in all those harbours, but seven boats are kept, which are at Ferryland. And years together in those above harbours have been forty sail of fishing ships; so your Lordships may plainly see the great decay of the noble fishery."

The colonists warned about the consequences of not being fortified and protected, for "...if your petitioners, having no fort, should also be void of a man of war [warship] to protect our fishery during the fishing season in the country, your petitioners will be most certainly ruined.

Map — Battleground for Two Nations. (Map: B.F.)

"We most humbly pray that a fort may be erected in Ferryland, to protect our fishery in the summer and to preserve from plundering and burning.... And that your Honours would be pleased to grant a man of war to come to Ferryland. And that the Captain may have your Honours orders to stay there in the harbour to protect our men until a fort can be finished."

They went on to suggest that not only was Ferryland an important place to defend but that it "may be made a good fortification at little charge." They concluded their petition with the assurance that "...if Ferryland be taken care of, it will much encourage both shipping and the inhabitants to resort thither, so that a beneficial trade may be supported..."

Nothing was done about the requests and pleas of the inhabitants of Ferryland to fortify their settlement for four years and by then it was too late once again. In the winter of 1708-09 the French from Placentia once again launched an attack on the English settlements of the Avalon. Once again the attack came in the dead of winter and once again overland, but this time not from Placentia but from the direction of St. John's. The French had gone directly there and had successfully taken that town and then turned their attention to the settlements along the Shore. But this time they would not take Ferryland and it remained the only English settlement in Newfoundland not to be captured that winter.

While the French Commander, St. Ovide, who had so easily captured Ferryland three years earlier was busy attacking St. John's and the other settlements to the north, he sent a company of troops under a Lt. Larond with a party of Micmac Indians to capture Ferryland. There Larond found the inhabitants of the settlement forted-up on Bouys Island behind a makeshift earthworks and palisade and they refused to surrender. They showed they were willing to fight and were so confident of their position that they even refused a flag of truce to land on the island to talk.

Larond had no ship or cannon with him since he had come overland and probably expected the settlement to be undefended as it had been three years earlier. He could well see that any attempt he might make to land a boat at any of the few landing sites on the island could be easily repulsed by the small arms fire of the defenders. He spent two weeks trying to cajole or convince the defenders to surrender, then had to break off his siege when he ran short of supplies. He plundered what belongings the settlers had not carried onto the island with them, and once again put the settlement to the torch before he departed.

This time, however, none of the colonists had been captured, ransomed, or deported, and they had saved most of their belongings and livestock. Thus they could begin rebuilding at once.

British Troops: Sat watchfully as the French settlers at Placentia evacuated their colony. Unlike the settlers of Avalonia they were allowed to keep their property, did not see their homes burned, and were transported to a place of their choosing. (Photo: Parks Canada. Castle Hill Nat'l Historic Park.)

In 1713 the latest war between France and England came to an end with the Treaty of Utrecht which saw the French forever banned from settling in Newfoundland again or building any kind of fortifications there. The Treaty of Utrecht was probably one of the most important events to occur in the history of the Colony of Avalonia. It banished the French from Placentia, the back yard of Baltimore's colony, and more importantly banished them from the coastal fishing waters of Placentia Bay and the southern bays of the Shore and the Avalon Peninsula.

Not only did the colonists of Ferryland not have to fear further attacks from the French colony at Placentia, but they could now freely fish in the waters the French had used. Their economic prosperity was largely improved with their free access to the bountiful fish stocks off the southeast coast and on the Grand Banks where the French had swarmed for the past fifty years. Ferryland and the Colony of Avalonia enjoyed a prolonged period of success in the fishery that lasted long into the eighteenth century.

PROFILE — D'Iberville: Soldier Son of New France

Pierre le Moyne Sieur d'Iberville is considered by many to be the finest soldier-son of New France during the century of conflict between France and England for possession of North America during the last half of the seventeenth and first half of the eighteenth centuries. He was born in Montreal on July 16, 1661, twenty years after his father had arrived there from Dieppe with his grandfather who had been a tavern keeper. He was the third son in a family of eleven brothers and three sisters, from which nearly half the brothers would become soldiers of New France.

At the early age of twelve he was introduced to what would become his way of life — the soldiering way. In 1673 his father took him and his two older brothers on an expedition with Governor Frontenac of Quebec into hostile Iroquois country to establish a fort. Soon after he was sent to France where he spent twelve years in the French Navy. When he returned home to Canada he began the exploits that saw him become as good a soldier as he was a sailor.

He was not long back in Quebec when his two older brothers asked him to join them on an expedition to destroy the English trading posts in Hudson's Bay. Their expedition left Montreal in mid-March and travelled up the Ottawa River to first strike the Hudson's Bay Company post at Fort Hayes. When the sleep roused English traders rushed from their blockhouse they found themselves staring into the muskets of d'Iberville's *coureur de bois*. The bloodless capture of Fort Hayes was quickly followed by the capture of Fort Rupert about forty miles farther north on the shore of the great bay that carried the name of the English fur trading company. A ship at anchor in the bay also had to be taken and Pierre le Moyne, as the sailor among the d'Ibervilles, was given that task. Under cover of darkness he silently boarded the ship and quickly had the surprised crew in irons. The ship yielded an unexpected prize, the Governor of the Company of Gentlemen who ran the Hudson's Bay Company.

The capture of Fort Albany on the Southern Shore of the bay proved more difficult as the English were now aware of the French attacks. D'Iberville's naval skills were once again called upon and using the captured English ship he began firing on the fort with the ship's cannons setting it afire and forcing the occupants to surrender within an hour.

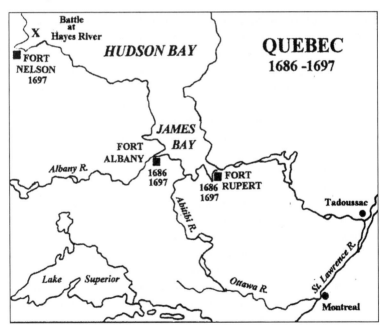

Map — D'Iberville's Raids in Hudson's Bay: 1686–1697. (Map: B.F.)

In 1690, d'Iberville again accompanied his brothers on a campaign, this time into the New England colonies. The severe winter weather and the preparedness of the English settlements forced them to retreat without destroying all their objectives. They did succeed in attacking the town of Schenectady where the trail weary Huron Indians with them went on a rampage, killing women and children along with the men who tried to defend them. Most of those spared owed their lives to the intervention of the D'Iberville brothers.

Soldier of the Montreval Regiment. Many of these soldiers, stationed in Quebec to guard New France, took part in the wars in Newfoundland. From 1696 to 1710 they were more than once unwelcome visitors at Ferryland as they sacked and burned Calvert's colony. (Photo: BF-NMM.)

By 1696, Governor Frontenac of New France had decided to rid North America of the British presence. But before he attacked the New England colonies he wanted the island of Newfoundland firmly in his hands. His Lieutenant-Governor there, Sieur de Brouillon, was having little success in completing the job so Frontenac decided to send him some competent and experienced help in the person of Pierre d'Iberville.

D'Iberville arrived in Newfoundland with a force of 120 French-Canadian *coureur de bois* and Abnaki and Micmac Indians with orders to destroy every English settlement on the Avalon Peninsula. During the winter of 1696–97, he did a relentless, thorough job of razing everything that was British on the Island's east coast.

When he left Newfoundland in the spring of 1697 he had captured and destroyed twenty-seven English settlements and outports on the Avalon Peninsula, killed 200 of the settlers, and taken more than 700 as prisoners. He devastated the English fishery in the colony and was preparing to attack the Bonavista Peninsula when he was recalled to Quebec.

The English had retaken their forts in Hudson's Bay and Frontenac wanted them back. In September of 1697, d'Iberville anchored his ship *Pelican* in the mouth of the Hayes River where he was soon attacked by three British warships. Nearly half of his 150 man crew was sick from the long voyage north and his 44 gun ship was up against 124 guns on the British ships. Still, he decided to fight.

He quickly showed his skill as a seaman and soon had two of the British ships disabled. He then duelled shot for shot with the remaining British ship for over an hour, taking heavy damage from the outnumbering guns of the Royal Navy vessel. Its captain at one point in the brisk exchange, appeared on the deck of his ship, raised a glass of wine in toast to the determined d'Iberville and asked for his surrender. D'Iberville drank his own toast to the British captain and promptly declined his request. The two captains continued their duel until a sudden wind change put d'Iberville in a position to fire broadside into his enemy. The result was sending the British ship to the bottom.

From Hudson's Bay d'Iberville went on to the Caribbean to contest the British there. He founded the Colony of Louisiana and its capitol, Biloxi (present-day Mobile, Alabama). From there he went on to fight campaigns in the West Indies, sacking the British colonies of Nevis and St. Christopher. During this expedition he contracted yellow fever and died of the disease at Havana, Cuba on July 9, 1706 just one week short of his forty-fifth birthday.

CHAPTER VII

The Masterless Men
of Ferryland

Ｔhe Seven Years War which once again saw the threat of the French in Newfoundland ended in 1762 when the last French invasion of Newfoundland was repulsed by the British at St. John's in September of that year. Ferryland and the Colony of Avalonia had also been threatened but was successfully defended by the women of the Bouys Island. With the French forever banished from North America with their loss of New France, most believed that they had seen the last of their almost 150 years of strife and warfare. Peace however, was short-lived and within a dozen years the English settlements in Newfoundland were once again under attack.

This time it was not the French who threatened them but their only recently allied British comrades of New England, the American colonists who rose up in rebellion against their British overlords in 1775. The American Revolution brought raids by the Yankee Privateers as they came to be called, and Ferryland did not escape their forays. The Privateers did little or no damage to the settlement of Ferryland itself as the Americans were well-acquainted with the harbour and its defenses and were reluctant to try to capture or plunder it. Their raids did play havoc with the fishing ships, or bankers that went far offshore to catch their cod, from the settlement however, and the troublesome upstarts took many a crew and their cargo.

The real damage to Avalonia was done from within. To the planters of Ferryland it seemed that the only time the home Government was willing to pay any attention or offer them any protection was when their own interests in the colony were threatened. This time their fight was in New England and they had little time to worry about the few fishing ships that were being plundered in the coastal waters of Newfoundland.

The laws against permanent settlement on the island instigated by the English merchants and the stringent restrictions against those brave enough to resist them, left the settlers of the colony completely to their own resources. With no instated seat of Government or enforcement of due law and order except the seasonal surrogate courts of the Royal Navy, the colony was a wild east frontier where men often made their own laws and enforced them accordingly. Ferryland became a particular example of the wild east. Between the close of the Seven Years War and the commencement of the American Revolution, Ferryland, with the outports of the Colony of Avalonia, found itself with the opportunity to expand its fishery into the coves and bays that had once been contested by the French.

After 1762 the French had been forced to give up much of their Shore and fishing stations from Placentia Bay to Port aux Basques along the south coast. As a result, the English fishery greatly expanded as they began to catch the fish and supply the markets the French had fished and supplied for the past 100 years. This expansion required more labour and the English merchants looked to Ireland to supply it. From 1762 more and more Irish youngsters were brought to Newfoundland to work in the fishery.

By that year there were some 350 Irish settlers living along the Shore at Renews, Fermuse, Ferryland and Bay Bulls, with others scattered in the smaller outports of Witless Bay, Tors

Cove, Cape Broyle, Calvert and Aquaforte. But these Irish settlers were not for the most part planters or merchants. They were mostly indentured servants and youngsters as they were called, men who were contracted out to the fishery for a season, which meant they would spend two summers and a winter in the colony in the employ of their planter or merchant master before returning home.

Both living and working conditions were harsh and sometimes downright appalling. Most of the Irish were treated as second-class citizens and viewed by their employers as simply servants and bonded or even forced labourers. Many masters were unfair and unscrupulous in their dealings with these servants.

Between 1760 and 1790 Court Records are rife with cases of youngsters and indentured servants bringing suit against their employers for failure to pay wages, for wrongfully dismissing them on some false charge, or refusing to pay their return passage after their season was finished as was required by law.

Many won their cases but many more did not. As a result many youngsters found themselves stranded in *Talonvanish* — the far-off island of fish as they came to call Newfoundland. With no employment, no assistance, and no prospects, they began to band together in the settlements of the Southern Shore, living in shantytowns and surviving any way they could, which in most cases meant by means beyond the law.

By the mid 1700s the Irish population of the Avalon Peninsula from St. John's to Trepassey was about 1,500 while the English population in the same area numbered about 1,000. Most of the Irish were destitute and desperate. It was believed by the English settlers and the overseers that the shantytowns "were possessed and inhabited by Irish Roman Catholics...who entertain and keep in the country a great quantity of rogues and vagabonds to the great disturbance of the peace and danger to his Majesty's subjects' lives and to the exceeding great prejudice of the fishing trade."

Irish "Youngsters" indentured to the fishery of *Talonvanish* as they called Newfoundland, were in most cases not youngsters at all. Most were mature, robust men willing to take on hard work but were inexperienced in the trade and so the sobriquet. They signed on for the season —two summers and a winter, for which they were paid 18 pounds, about 200 dollars, for a year and a half's work. They were supplied their found, or board, but everything else they might require was "on tick" from his master or the fish merchant who bought his catch. Their life was a harsh and spartan one. Most found accommodations in the lofts of fish stores, or under fish flakes and stages, or built their own shacks or tilts. The lucky ones found lodging houses which cost them most of their pay by the end of their season. These star boarders were often referred to as dieters. For most of them it was a lean diet indeed. (Photo: Parks Canada. Signal Hill Nat'l Historic Park.)

The religious freedom, which Lord Baltimore had ideally and sincerely sought to found his Colony of Avalonia on, had not come to fruition. One hundred and fifty years after his dream of a New World of religious tolerance it still had not been achieved. Roman Catholics in Newfoundland, which meant mostly the Irish, still did not have the religious rights of their English cousins. They were still being referred to as "Papists" officially and as "popists" derisively. Ever since the time of the Cromwell Commonwealth 100 years earlier, the rights of Catholics had been suppressed both in Ireland and in Newfoundland. Priests were not permitted in the colony and public worship by Catholics was forbidden.

When English fishing admirals began to bring increasing numbers of Irish youngsters to Newfoundland in the early 1700s they were obliged to return with the same number on their homeward voyage. It was the British way of population control to ensure that the Irish would not grow larger in numbers in the colony than their own people. The law was aimed at the English merchants who once having gotten their service out of the youngsters refused to pay their return passage to Ireland as was required by law, leaving them destitute in the colony.

Tensions between the English and Irish had been growing steadily since 1762 and the last French invasion of the colony when dozens, if not hundreds of Irish had joined the French in their bid to take over the colony. Following the recapture of the colony by the British the governor had issued new orders concerning the Irish in Newfoundland. The orders read:

"No Papist servants, man or woman, shall remain at any place where they do not fish or serve during the summer preceding.
That not more than two Papist men shall dwell in one house during the winter except such that have a Protestant master.
That no Papist shall keep a public house or vend liquor for retail.
That no person shall keep dyeters [Irish fishermen] during the winter.
That all idle and disorderly men and women [Irish] be punished according to law and sent out of the country."

In 1770, the governor of the colony of Newfoundland, Lord Byron, (a relative of the famous poet) reissued the orders of 1762 regarding the Irish Papists with a couple of additions. "The masters of Irish servants," he decreed, "shall pay their passage home," and "That the children of Roman Catholics born in this country be baptized according to the law." [The Church of England].

In 1774 an incident occurred in St. John's that was to have severe consequences for the Irish settlers not only in that town but for Irish settlers all over the island. A band of ten Irishmen and one Irishwoman killed an English magistrate and the English inhabitants of the colony were outraged when they learned that the crime was not simply one committed during a robbery gone bad but that the murder had been premeditated.

As a result the governor severely curtailed the religious freedoms of the Irish in an attempt to force them to leave. Priests who had come to the colony incognito to serve the Irish in a kind of circuit church were hunted down and deported. People who had allowed their homes to be used to celebrate mass had their possessions seized, their property confiscated, and their homes burned or torn down.

These retaliations by the colonial administration and the further restrictions on the practice of the Catholic religion served to further increase the animosity between master and servant, Catholic and Protestant, and English and Irish. For many Irish youngsters the free life of a masterless man was an attractive alternative to the poverty and squalor of the fishing rooms in the settlements where they had no prospects whatsoever, and many headed out for the freedom they believed could be found among the Society of the Masterless Men.

It was into these times and circumstances that the legends of the Newfoundland outlaws were spawned — groups of runaways who, either cheated, mistreated, or abandoned, were left to their own devices to survive in a harsh and unforgiving land. Perhaps none gained more fame than the Masterless Men of the Butterpots of the Ferryland area of Baltimore's colony, led by a man named Peter Kerrivan.

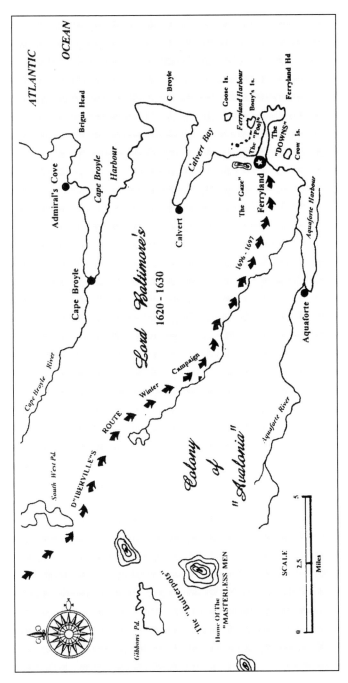

Map — Lord Baltimore's Colony. (Map: B.F.)

Half fact, half fiction, mixed with the mists and fogs of myth and legend, they were described by some as thieving, murdering outlaws and by others as championing Robin Hoods. In truth they were probably neither. No records exist telling that any of them were ever executed for murder or highway robbery, just as none tell that they "robbed from the rich to give to the poor." A few were apprehended and executed, but not for crimes against society, but for desertion from the Royal Navy or British army.

The legend of the Society of the Masterless Men may have more basis in fact than many believe. By the 1780s there was a growing movement in Ireland called the United Irishmen's Movement that aimed at uniting all Irishmen, regardless of religion in one cause — to rid Ireland of Englishmen. It was a secretive society and in colonial Newfoundland would have been outlawed as subversive or even downright treasonous. By the early 1790s the movement had developed into a Society with a blood oath and a highly rebellious philosophy.

The United Irish Society did develop in Newfoundland and culminated in the rising of 1,800 when Irish soldiers among the British garrison in St. John's rose up in mutiny. The mutiny was supposed to herald the start of a full-scale revolt, or rising, by the general population but when the muscle of the rising, the soldiers muskets, did not materialize in the force counted on, the rhetoric of the revolutionaries failed to sustain the general populace. By the late 1780s the United Irishmen's movement no doubt was known about in Newfoundland and may have had clandestine factions here at that time. The religious riots at Ferryland in the late 1780s seem to support this possibility and the Society of the Masterless Men may have been a euphemism for a precursor of the United Irishmen's Society. Indeed, remnants of the Society survive today, although with the much blander moniker of the Newfoundland Irish Association.

The country said to be the wilderness haunts of the Society of Masterless Men was the Butterpots, an isolated, rugged, and uncharted area some miles inland from Ferryland on the southern Avalon Peninsula. Dotted with lakes and connected by rivers and streams it proved to be very passable to those who came to know it, but for those who didn't, such as the Royal Navy parties who came to search for deserters, it proved to be a maze of bogs and barrens carpeted with a matting of what one observer called: "Newfoundland's most devilish specialty: matted dwarf spruce, three or four feet deep, too thick to walk through, and just a trifle too thin to walk over," what most Newfoundlanders today call tuckamore.

Just how Kerrivan, a seaman unaccustomed to life in the wilderness, learned his survival skills is an intriguing part of the story of the Masterless Men. Some have attributed it to their mingling with the native Beothuck Indians, and while this is remotely possible it is highly improbable given their character-istic intractable nature. It is more likely they acquired their wilderness skills from the Micmac Indians of Nova Scotia.

When the French established their colony at Placentia they brought with them a number of Micmac Indians from Acadia to hunt and trap for them in the hinterlands of the Avalon Peninsula west of Baltimore's colony at Ferryland. By the time of the outbreak of the wars between France and England at the turn of the eighteenth century their numbers had increased, and by 1707 there were about 150 of the Nova Scotia Indians in Newfoundland, many of them living on the French Islands of St. Pierre and Miquelon from where they made frequent excursions to the main island of Newfoundland to hunt and trap.

During the French winter attacks on the English settle-ments of Avalonia the Micmacs savagely plundered and their cruel slaughter of settlers so disgusted and angered their French benefactors that one Governor of Placentia, de Costabelle, ordered the Indians expelled from Newfoundland.

The Micmacs ignored the order, and while most of them sought refuge at St. Pierre and Miquelon, many stayed on the island of Newfoundland dispersing throughout the bays and coves of the western Avalon and in Placentia Bay. In all probability it was these Indian outlaws that Kerrivan and his outlaws encountered in the wilderness of Avalonia. Several of these Masterless Men were apprehended over the years and did suffer punishment for their crimes of theft and other unlawful acts, doled out in fines, floggings or transport — usually a one-way ticket to the penal colony of Australia.

The Society of the Masterless Men, as it came to be known, was begun around the year 1750 in or near Baltimore's colony at Ferryland by a young run-away from the Royal Navy named Peter Kerrivan. Unlike many of those who would join him, Kerrivan's crime was punishable by death. He was a deserter in time of war and not a civilian run-away from a master, which crime was not summarily punishable by the death penalty.

Kerrivan's Society of Masterless Men probably acquired its unique sobriquet from the fact that most of his gang was made up of civilian run-aways, indentured servants to the fishery who had left their masters before their season was up or had been cheated or abandoned by them. It was these kinds of desperadoes who flocked to Kerrivan's gang of Masterless Men.

Kerrivan himself had left his masters in a port somewhere along the Shore with a couple of shipmates and struck out into the wilds to avoid capture. The western hinterland of Baltimore's Avalonia was such country and it is said that for perhaps as long as fifty years he and his men eluded the authorities while surviving in the wilderness around the Butterpot Barrens. Kerrivan himself was never captured and is said to have died at the Butterpot Mountain where, some claim, he is buried.

Butterpot Mountain, which is actually a group of three or four hills prominent on the landscape, is about ten miles behind Ferryland west of the settlement. It was for Kerrivan the finest lookout he could have found in the entire area of the interior of the southern Avalon Peninsula. From it he could observe the harbour at Ferryland as well as St. Mary's Bay to the south, and even as far north as Conception and Trinity Bays. In the isolation and remoteness of the Butterpots, Kerrivan's Society grew through the years.

The Masterless Men of the Butterpots: Learned to live off the land in the wilderness of the Butterpots area of the Avalon Peninsula several miles inland from the settlement of Ferryland. They hunted, trapped, and fished in the interior and traded with the nearby settlements for other staples. In exchange for fresh country meat, caribou and their hides, they bartered with the settlers for salt pork and mutton, flour and vegetables like potatoes, cabbages, and turnips which would keep over winter, and tea and molasses. They also got their supplies of powder and shot from the settlers which allowed them to continue their hinterland lifeway. When trade was not possible it is said, they resorted to stealthy raids when they took what they wanted or needed. But it is said they never took from the poorer fishermen or planters. This gained them a reputation as a sort of band of Robin Hoods although it cannot be said with the same certainty that they gave to the poor. If one thing seemed to be certain in the philosophy of the Masterless Men, it was that they believed that charity began at home. (Photo: Courtesy *The Newfoundland Quarterly.*)

In the years when the French still controlled the coasts they were forced to vacate after 1762, many Irish run-aways found refuge with them. They were cousins in a kind of way, based on their Catholic religion and the fact that both their nations were almost continuously at war with the English. By the time of the formation of the Masterless Men, dozens, if not hundreds of run-aways may have taken up residence along the French Shore where they made their way into the backwoods to learn the wilderness skills of the Indians.

If Kerrivan made contact with these men he would have had decades of practical experience to draw upon without having to overcome the slowly learned hurdles of the barriers of language and customs.

However he and his men learned the art of survival, they learned it well. In the more than half a century that they were believed to live in the wilderness few of them were ever apprehended. In the raw hinterland Kerrivan and his followers enjoyed a freedom few of their compatriots in the coastal communities would ever dream of having. They had no masters to mistreat, cheat, punish, or impoverish them. Neither did they have to suffer the religious scorn and prejudice which was still very real in the settlements.

Colonial authorities considered the Irish to be the cause of all the discontent and lawlessness in the colony. In an attempt at intimidation, most settlements, which contained large proportions of Irish in the populations, were furnished with gibbets, stocks, and public whipping posts. Ferryland itself was supplied with a gibbet and three flogging posts. It was an obvious warning to the settlers that they were not to aid or abet the Society of Masterless Men.

By the early 1780s the notoriety and numbers of Kerrivan's gang had steadily grown until the Masterless Men became a legend in their own time. The Society had come to be viewed as a threat to British authority in the colony and officials directed the Royal Navy to go in search of the band, bring them back to justice and make an example of them by hanging them all.

Such a task did not prove to be an easy one. The expedition took time to ready and during that time Kerrivan learned from his contacts in Ferryland when it would occur. He prepared for it by having his men cut numerous blind trails into the wilderness, which ended in broad soggy bogs or thickets of dense woods.

The Royal Navy search party penetrated to the Butterpots, but when they reached there they found the hideout deserted. Kerrivan and his Masterless Men had dispersed into the forests and barrens north and west of their hideaway. The Navy Lieutenant and his Royal Marines stumbled around in the wilderness for a few days just as Kerrivan had planned then finally gave up the search.

They returned to the Butterpots hideout and went through the collection of tilts of the outlaws but found nothing of value, everything worthwhile having been taken along by outlaws. They burned the tilts to the ground and returned to Ferryland empty-handed without having even seen their quarry. At least three more expeditions were sent in search of the Masterless Men but all were unsuccessful in capturing any of the elusive outlaws. Three times the tilts were burned to the ground and three times they were rebuilt. It was almost ten years before any of the Masterless Men were brought to justice.

The Society, although living the wild life, had not completely forsaken civilized life. In their clandestine visits to the nearby settlements of the Shore to trade and barter they also found some companionship. A good number of them took wives from the settlements, one of them said to be Kerrivan himself. Just how much contact or how much influence the Masterless Men had with the settlements of the Shore is not known for certain, but the authorities were convinced that they had far too much.

In 1788-9, Ferryland and its nearby outports were the scene of rowdy winter riots. Just what involvement, if any, Kerrivan's men had in the fracas is uncertain, but it is clear from the records that some of them at least had an indirect part in the disturbances if not a direct one.

That winter saw religious riots — not as might be expected between Protestants and Catholics, but between rival factions of Catholics led by two priests: Father James O'Donel and Father Patrick Power. It is not exactly clear what touched off the shenanigans but a likely cause was the appointment of O'Donel as the official shepherd of the Irish flock in Newfoundland and his recognition as such by the British authorities.

O'Donel had been having trouble with rogue priests since his arrival in the colony as the Catholic Church's official head clergyman and had been doing his best to rein them in and bring them under his authority. These rogue priests had been moving around in the colony to avoid being apprehended and deported by the authorities. While they moved about to conduct the legitimate business of the Church they also espoused their own personal philosophies, some of which included revolt against the British authorities. O'Donel opposed their personal preachings and when his authority was challenged in Ferryland by Power and his supporters things came to a violent head.

The exact details of the riots are cloudy but the disturbances proved serious enough to warrant the full attention of the colonial authorities. The trouble occurred when two rival factions of Irishmen in Ferryland lined up in the dispute between their priests, O'Donel and Power. The Irish youngsters had brought their homegrown differences from Ireland across the big pond with them during their migrations of the past thirty years or so. It seems there was a long-time Provincial rivalry between the Provinces of Leinster and Munster in southern Ireland and by 1788 many men from both Provinces had found their way to Ferryland and the nearby outports. It appears the Wexford-Leinster men supported the rogue cleric Father Power while the Waterford-Munster men backed Father O'Donel — as he was the duly appointed head of the Church in the colony — in their holy feud.

The interior barrens of what is today the Avalon Wilderness Area is a windswept area of rock strewn barrens dotted with marshes and bogs and drokes of woods which made it ideal habitat for the Masterless Men's main food supply of fresh country meat, the Newfoundland caribou, as well as provided good winterhouse campsites and rough country over which no track or trail could be easily found. (Photo: B.F.)

In the winter a fracas broke out between a gang of the Leinster men led by a character named Fogarty from County Wexford and a bunch of the Munster boys. Apparently it was not the only donnybrook throughout the winter and colonial officials had their suspicions that Kerrivan's Society of Masterless Men had more than a little to do with the distur-bances, if not instigating them, then at least encouraging them, given their dislike of the British authorities. Father O'Donel, who was doing all he could to cooperate with the British authorities to ensure his precarious foothold in the colony was not jeopardized, found he had a big problem when the governor of Ferryland, Robert Carter, who was also the Admiralty Judge for the district as well as one of the most important and successful fish merchants and businessmen of the area, sided with Father Power and his Leinster men.

Governor Carter also had the support of Captain Edward Pellew of the Royal Navy who was also Surrogate Judge of the Colonial Court for the Ferryland area. Pellew was noted to be "a most bitter enemy to Roman Catholics" and personally believed that they should all be banished from the colony. Pellew informed the colonial governor, Admiral Sir Mark Milbanke, of the affair in a letter which O'Donel later reported on to his superiors in Ireland. "The letter [Pellew's report] was not only read in the courthouse," O'Donel wrote, "where the Surrogate [Pellew] denounced Pope, Popery, Priests and Priestcraft, and in an extasy [sic: ecstasy] blessed his happy constitution that was cleanly purged from such knavery.... This Surrogate...closed his surrogation to the Admiral [Governor Milbanke] with the modest request that Power and I should be turned out of the country and that circular letters ought to be sent to all the magistrates if any more priests arrived to ship them off immediately, and in his opinion no priest should be left but where there was a garrison to keep them in awe."

Pellew's report to the governor got the desired reaction and action. When Milbanke returned to the colony in the spring of 1789 he sent Captain Pellew in HMS *Winchelsea* to Ferryland to quell the disturbances, warn the priests, and hunt down the Masterless Men. The governor sent orders to the Magistrates of Ferryland concerning the priests. "As I am authorized by my Commission," he wrote, "to administer and give or cause to be administered or given the oath...to the security of His Majesty's person and Gov't to all and every person as I shall think fit who shall at any time or times pass into this island or shall be resident or abiding here. I must desire you that you shall not on any account whatsoever suffer either of the R.C. priests at Ferryland to exercise the duties of their function until they shall have taken and submitted to the same oath of which you will not fail to provide me with a copy."

O'Donel convinced his supporters that an oath of allegiance to the Crown in no way reflected on their religious beliefs but getting the rogue priest and his followers to do the same O'Donel believed might be a little more difficult. He could see all the work he had being doing for the past five years since his arrival in the colony to help spread the Catholic faith coming undone.

Captain Pellew then turned his attentions to the Masterless Men. Perhaps because of the ill feelings that had surfaced as a result of the recent riots he learned the identities of several of the members of the Society and determined to capture them and make an example of them. He had come to Ferryland armed with the authority to deal with the outlaws to the utmost limits of the law – which meant he had leave to hang them on the spot. Over the next year he made a concerted effort to track the Society members and was successful in capturing four of them near the Butterpots. They may have been stragglers cut off from the main band or even escaped convicts from St. John's but Pellew was determined to have his examples.

In March of 1791 a Surrogate Court was convened in Ferryland to deal with the riots of 1788-9 and the like disturbances of the following winter. Along with the local magistrates Captain Pellew, whom the colonial officials considered had done an admirable job of dealing with the situation, also sat as a Surrogate Judge. On March 31 he read charges against

137 men of Ferryland and the surrounding areas and convicted them all of "riotous and unlawful assembly." They were all sentenced to pay fines and most were ordered transported, that is to be returned to Ireland if not to some penal colony for punishment. As many as 200 more were convicted in absentia and their sentences were to be "executed if they return." Court documents record that some of the in absentia convicted were members of the Masterless Men as a notation beside their names read "Run-Away."

It is said that the four hapless Masterless Men that fell into Pellew's hands were sentenced to hang and the execution was carried out aboard the captain's ship in Ferryland harbour. The men were hanged from the yardarm of the vessel in a public spectacle as a warning and a lesson to all who would contest or challenge the authority of the British Crown in the colony.

With the close of these proceedings the lure of the Masterless Men became a little less alluring. The loss of some 350 men from Ferryland and the other communities along the Shore was a great deterrent to any who might have considered joining the Society. There were other incentives not to go the wild route also.

The tenuous religious freedom that Catholics enjoyed was given a guarantee in 1791 when a proper Judicial system was set up in Newfoundland with civilian judges presiding from a Supreme Colonial Court that took the administration of the law out of the hands of the governors, who often set their own rules and meted out their own kind of justice. Father O'Donel was greatly relieved that year when Judge John Reeves was appointed Chief Justice of the Newfoundland Court. Reeves assured O'Donel "that the Catholic Church in Newfoundland would be unmolested."

With the assurance of religious freedom and a steady progress being made to make settlement legal in the colony, and with the establishment of a fair and equitable Judiciary in the colony, many of the Irish transients and youngsters felt that they could even look forward to the possibility of making a living for themselves in the colony. These incentives, although scarcely attainable for most, saw many a potential recruit for the Society of Masterless Men opting for the more civilized and less risky life than that of an outlaw among a vanishing brotherhood.

By the early 1800s the Masterless Men had become more of a memory that a reality, if indeed such a Society ever actually existed at all. Those who believe they did also believe they left a legacy more positive than negative. Their fifty years of traversing the interior of the Avalon Peninsula blazed and carved trails so well travelled that they were considered to be some of the first roads in the colony which were expanded and improved in the nineteenth century, and in some cases were still in use into the twentieth century.

Some of their roads crisscrossed the southern Avalon from Ferryland to Placentia to St. Mary's Bay in the south, and north to Trinity Bay with a terminus at Dildo. It is thought some of their tracks were used and improved by the early twentieth century Newfoundland Government for use by their mail carriers who in the early days transported the mail on foot or by dogsled.

Some legends still persist that a handful of the Masterless Men persisted well into the 1800s, mostly those who had been tried and convicted in absentia and had never returned to the settlements for fear of capture.

As for the grand patriarch of the Society, Peter Kerrivan, it is said he never gave up his wild life in the interior that had been his home and sanctuary for half a century. Some say he lived to a grand old age and died at the Butterpots on some unknown date and is buried there at some unknown site.

It is also believed that Kerrivan left four sons and several daughters who eventually integrated into the settlements along the Shore and over the generations left descendants who still survive today as a testimony to the adventurous, free-willed spirit of the "old Man of the Mountain."

Time may never reveal the true extent of the facts or fictions behind the legend of the Society of the Masterless Men of Ferryland, but it is enough to know that their spirit has endured in the people of the Shore for 250 years.

PROFILE — Bouys Island: Ferryland Fortress

Isle aux Bois as it was named by the French, later Anglicized to Bouys Island, (various spellings have been used including Buoys and the more familiar Boys of today) was a natural fortress waiting to be discovered. Unfortunately for the original Planters of Baltimore's Colony of Avalonia in Ferryland, this fact was not observed until almost 100 years after the settlement had been founded, and only after the settlement had been attacked, sacked, plundered and depopulated four times by warfare, pirating and privateering.

Lying about three-quarters of a mile from the Pool, the heart of Ferryland harbour, and extending its protective chain of shoals across the harbour, it is distant only about one-quarter mile from the headlands of the Downs, another site which was also found to be easily defended.

The island, although relatively flat and treeless, has steep rising cliffs and a rocky shoreline with only two or three places that offer a precarious landing site. But it wasn't until the settlement of Ferryland had been attacked and plundered three times in 50 years that the defensive potential of Bouys Island was recognized

Lord Baltimore, who established the settlement, had fortified the inner harbour around the Pool but had failed to see the strategic potential of the island and had not fortified it. His inner harbour defenses failed to defend the settlement against pirate and buccaneer raids. Even Sir David Kirke with all his military savvy failed to see the value of the island as a defensive position. It took the settlers themselves who had lived through three invasions by the French to realize the defensive importance of Bouys Island.

It was left to the fishermen and planters of Ferryland to discover the usefulness of the island for defense and its potential as a fortress. After being attacked three times and sacked by the French between 1696 and 1705, the settlers of Ferryland finally discovered the defensive capability of the island in the winter of 1709 when the French once again threatened the settlement. Instead of waiting to be taken prisoner and deported, the settlers forted-up on the island and successfully resisted the French attack. Their victory so buoyed their confidence to be able to defend themselves that they respectfully declined an offer by the king to be relocated to some safer place in the spring of 1709.

Some forty "masters of families and inhabitants of the Island of Bouys [Ferryland] in Newfoundland" wrote her Majesty Queen Anne in May of 1709 to thank her for her offer "and support to transport us to your Excellency's government, which in all humility we acknowledge to be an infinite favour and with all submission acknowledge our gratitude and thankfulness.

"But, as hath pleased God of His infinite mercy and goodness to protect and defend us against our enemies in two different assaults, we hope by the same providence to defend ourselves against all their assaults, being fully resolved to maintain this our Island to the last extremity for Her Majesty's honour, and our nation's interest and shall be ready, if required, to act offensively against our enemies, to the end that they may be totally rooted out of this country."

The settler's willingness to go on the offensive for the nation was far more than the nation was willing to do to defend them. Their repeated pleas and petitions to have the

Island fortified with gun batteries and a garrison of troops fell on deaf ears and were not acted on for more than thirty years until the outbreak of the War of Austrian Succession in 1742.

Bouys Island. Guarding the entrance to Ferryland harbour about halfway out on the "Downs," the island when fortified was a fortress, which could not be bypassed. From the mid 1700s until the early 1800s its heavily armed batteries succeeded in deterring any attempt at "invasion" of the Colony of Avalonia. (Photo: Courtesy of K. Mooney, *Southern Scenics.*)

After the Treaty of Utrecht in 1713 the strategic importance of the island became apparent to some of those in authority, but during the following twenty-five years Ferryland enjoyed a period of peace and nothing was done to fortify the place. But war did come again between England and France in 1742.

The British once again scrambled to consolidate their defenses in Newfoundland. Four settlements were considered to be crucial to their retaining possession of their colony of Newfoundland, and Ferryland was one of them. In 1743, Captain Smith of the Royal Navy realized the military importance of the island and had a battery of eight guns erected at the southern end of the harbour. He had a barracks built and had it permanently garrisoned by regular troops of the 45th Regiment of Foot and the Royal Artillery.

During the next three years two more batteries were erected on the island. The Southwest Battery was constructed in 1745 and consisted of six guns and the following year the Northwest Battery was built containing four guns. By 1747 Bouys Island had become a veritable fortress which housed a tiny village. It had two Officer's barracks, four soldier's barracks, and four or five sheds and outhouses used to store gunpowder, cannon shot and other provisions and supplies. A natural spring was found and welled-up to supply fresh water. The fortification also sported a cookhouse and a smithy to supply the needs of the armoury.

The island was so heavily fortified and well defended that the French did not attempt to attack it until almost twenty years later when they once again invaded Newfoundland. In 1762 a French force sailed into Newfoundland waters intent on capturing the colony and holding it ransom as a bargaining chip in their ongoing treaty discussions concerning the fate of the Northern American continent. In the early summer of 1762 a French fleet captured St. John's and nearby outports then turned their sails south to the other settlements along the Shore.

Of the three batteries on Bouys Island, only one of them ever fired its guns in defense of Ferryland. And they were said to have been fired not by gunmen but by "gunwomen." When word reached Ferryland of the French invasion the governor of the settlement, Robert Carter, moved all the people, estimated to be between two and three hundred at that time, onto Bouy's Island to prepare to defend the settlement against attack. Carter and the men went off towards St. John's to help in the fight there leaving the women of Ferryland to defend their home-town.

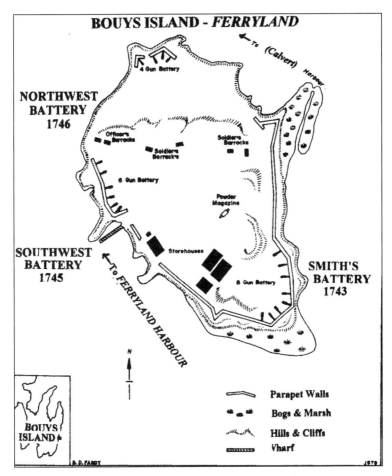

Map — Bouys Island, Ferryland. (Map: B.F.)

While the men were gone two French warships showed up off the harbour and attempted to enter. Carter's wife rallied the Ferryland women and they opened fire on the French ships. Some of their cannon shots hit one of them, damaging it badly, and both then withdrew, realizing they could not force the harbour against the guns of Bouys Island.

After 1762, the defenses of the island fortress were allowed to fall into disrepair as the military garrison was withdrawn and the island was used by the governor of Ferryland,

Robert Carter, as fishing premises since Carter had apparently "bought" the island some years earlier. The defensive capabilities of the island were needed once again with the outbreak of the American Revolution to guard the settlement of Ferryland against attacks by Yankee Privateers. In 1776 the decaying cannons were replaced and new ones mounted on the island as well as on the nearby smaller Goose Island. However, the guns were never needed and allowed to again fall into disrepair after the war ended.

The fortifications of Bouys Island were forgotten again for another thirty years until the War of 1812 when the batteries were refitted and a new one constructed on the "Downs" at Stakes Point directly across from the island to guard both sides of the entrance to the harbour. The fortifications were abandoned for the final time at the end of that war in 1815. For a time the abandoned barracks and other buildings were used by fishermen as summer fishing cottages and to store their gear.

Bouys Island and the Downs: The island (at centre) when fortified could successfully guard the entrance to the Pool area of Ferryland harbour (hook-shaped area at right). (Photo: Courtesy of K. Mooney, *Southern Scenics*.)

When the buildings disappeared the island was used to graze the sheep of the town as indeed it still is today. The building ruins, the abandoned cannon, and the flattened well all lie half-buried today in the ground and beneath the grass, left behind after 250 years. Not left behind however, is the rich history and legacy of the island and a settlement that survived privation, hardship, wars, and destruction, and still survives as one of the oldest settlements in Newfoundland and the new World.

Stakes Point Pass Battery. This Battery was set up during the war of 1812 on the "Downs" to guard against attack by "Yankee Privateers." Its situation in conjunction with the batteries on Bouys Island allowed the guns of both positions to direct a devastating crossfire on any enemy ship trying to enter Ferryland harbour. (Photo: B.F.)

CHAPTER VIII

The Changing Times —
The Good, The Bad...

The turn of the nineteenth century saw a great boom in the economy of Newfoundland due to the fishery and the Colony of Avalonia shared in the prosperity. England and France were once again at war on the European continent and in twelve years England would also be embroiled in war in America at the same time as they entered the war of 1812 with the United States. The booming war economy saw a huge increase in the demand for salt cod and the Newfoundland fishery saw a great need for more labour to keep up to the demands. More and more Irish youngsters were brought out to the island to meet the labour demand.

The fishing settlement of Ferryland once again became an important fishing port and centre of commerce. Wages for youngsters doubled. Many of them now believed they could see their way free from the work-in-debt syndrome. By 1815 and the end of the Napoleonic Wars England had opened the floodgates and allowed ever more Irish to immigrate to Newfoundland.

Most of them settled along the Southern Shore and in St. Mary's Bay which area became known as the Cape Shore, while many more occupied the former French premises in Placentia Bay. In truth, all of the east coast of the Avalon peninsula from St. John's to Trepassey Bay and west across St. Mary's Bay and north into Placentia Bay as far as the settlement of Placentia became Irish territory.

With the influx of immigrants the British Government was obliged to relent on its "no settlement" policy and began to give grants of land to those who wanted to settle on the island in the hopes that they would become self-sufficient, productive colonists of the British empire.

There was a dramatic change in the economic and social facade of Avalonia. Free men found themselves allowed to take up land holdings, earn wages, and even compete with the merchant princes of England. The whole fabric of Newfoundland society changed. Gone were the days of the dictatorial merchants and the heavy-handed fishing admirals. But this new-found freedom and undreamed of land ownership left some heady with the reality and some became as heavy-handed as those they hoped to displace.

One new landowner in Avalonia jealously guarded his grant of real estate. He posted a notice warning all trespassers of dire consequences in a St. John's newspaper on August 20, 1813: "Whereas certain evil disposed persons break through the Fence, and enter on the farm of the undersigned, treading the grass, digging and destroying the potatoes, and also breaking over the Garden Fence, steal from thence vegetables. Other persons not EVIL MINDED, may inadvertently trespass thereon, TO THEM this caution is particularly directed, that ONE MONTH after this date, AND EVER AFTER, man-traps and spring guns will be placed in the garden fields, and potato ground of the said farm; and they are requested to consider, that their limbs with their lives, may be lost by those terrible instruments of punishment. Thus cautioned, it is presumed none but Rogues or Fools will be taken, whose punishment no man can pity, and whose loss none will lament."

As settlement increased along the Shore the once flourishing bank fishery began to rapidly decline in the face of the growing sedentary fishery. Small operators and independent fishermen supplied the markets from an inshore fishery and by 1830 there were only two bankers operating out of Ferryland, in addition to four large vessels and about a dozen foreign ships. The day of the small boat and the inshore fishery had arrived.

By the late 1830s the English fishing ships had all but disappeared from Newfoundland waters. Most of the large English trading companies had pulled out of the colony as most trade in fish could be supplied by the Newfoundland companies for much less cost. The trade was carried out by small local firms based in St. John's and Ferryland, which by now had become the second capital of the fish trade in Newfoundland.

The Fishery at Avalonia had changed little in the 200 years after Baltimore established his colony there. When the banker ship arrived in Ferryland (top right) its bank boats landed the catch at the stage (centre) where the fish was made. It was headed, gutted and "soundboned" (centre of stage) then packed in salt in alternating layers of salt and split fish (left of stage) where it was left several days to cure. Then it was carried to the landwash (beach) where it was washed to remove the caked salt (centre bottom) and finally laid out on the flakes to dry (bottom right). A byproduct of the catch was cod liver oil. The cod livers were dumped into a vat of water where they decayed into an oil. The vat was then drained into two casks: one collected the blood filled water that floated on top of the oil and the other the oil which was poured into casks for transport to England. (Photo: the *Herman Moll Map — 1710.* PAC.)

In Ferryland the breach left by the withdrawal of the English companies was filled by local firms such as James Carter, John White, Felix Hare, and John Morry who all became successful fish merchants through the fist half of the nineteenth century.

But just as prosperity seemed to be beckoning the fishermen and settlers of Avalonia, nature took a hand, perhaps coupled with changing technology. The fishery saw successive failures from the 1840s to the late 1860s. Some attributed this to the "scarcity of fish and the foulness of the weather," but others claimed that the "catch of fish was good for the small boats but poor for the larger western boats" and allowed that this decline was due in part to the use of the cod seine. The industrialization of the fishery had emerged just as it had in all other aspects of trade and commerce. The Industrial Revolution had arrived in Newfoundland.

The demographic and social structure of the Colony of Avalonia also changed throughout the century in a slow and almost natural progression. From about 500 people in 1830 Ferryland grew to a population of nearly 700 by the mid-1880s. This population was predominantly Irish-born in the 1830s but by the 1880s was predominantly Newfoundland born of Irish immigrant parentage.

Before the large-scale immigration of Irish into the Ferryland area in the early 1800s the area also had a large proportion of Church of England families. By the mid-1880s the majority of people living there were of the Roman Catholic faith.

The decrease in the number of Church of England families in the area and the increase in the number of Catholics had been attributed by some to be due to interfaith marriages. The Church of England Bishop, the Reverend Field, visited Ferryland around 1850 and reported: "All the Protestants in the place [Ferryland] except two or three sick persons, were present at the service.... An influential inhabitant [originally of Aquaforte]...has lately conformed to the Roman Catholic faith, and has used his utmost endeavours to induce his large family to follow his example."

By the end of the 1880s, over 500 of the town's 700 people were Roman Catholic and by the turn of the twentieth century only seventeen families in Ferryland were recorded as being members of the Church of England.

Holy Trinity Church. was built in the early 1860s. By then religious tolerance of Roman Catholics in the Colony of Newfoundland had increased to the point that the Catholic Church was given permission to build its own churches. Any others built before circa 1850 were considered to be chapels. The Reverend Bishop Mullock chose five sites in Newfoundland, in which to erect houses of worship, one of which was Ferryland. It opened its doors to the congregation in 1865. The church still stands today in Ferryland after 140 years. The stone structure was originally called the Church of the Holy Family but had its name changed in the 1920s to Holy Trinity Church. In the late 1990s the church was given historical status and funding was granted to begin restoration. It remains largely unchanged on the outside except for the removal several years ago of the bell tower due to its deteriorated state. (Photo: Newfoundland and Labrador Heritage Site [Hereinafter NLHS] MUN-CNS.)

Though the natural progression saw Avalonia become predominantly Roman Catholic the signs were slow in coming. It was not until the 1860s that the Catholic community in Newfoundland received permission to build churches. Bishop Thomas Mullock was allowed to build five churches in the colony and one of the sites he chose was Ferryland. In 1863 the cornerstone was laid for the first Catholic church to be built in Ferryland. The church was built of stone quarried from Stone Island at the mouth of Calvert (Caplin Cove) Bay and was one of only five stone churches built during the day on the island. Today it is the only one that survives. Christened the Church of the Holy Family when it was opened in 1865 it later had its name changed to Holy Trinity Church in the 1920s.

By the late 1800s the growing number of local entrepreneurs had succeeded in securing their credit, supplies, and markets for their salt fish which was the main source of livelihood for the Ferryland fishermen. As the second capital of the fishery in the colony it soon found that many ships went on to St. John's to land their catches when the weather made landing at Ferryland a chancy business especially when the town was shrouded in fog.

This situation prompted the local merchants to band together and propose the construction of a lighthouse at Ferryland Head on the Downs, which task was undertaken in 1870. The light went on in 1871 but despite this modern safety measure Ferryland was the site of several tragic shipwrecks in the following years.

The fishery continued to have its ups and downs into the twentieth century but Ferryland maintained its steady population. Around the turn of the century the large trading company of Goodridge and Sons of St. John's which had branches all along the Shore and in St. Mary's and Placentia Bays was liquidated and its Southern Shore interests bought out by the successful Carter merchant family of Ferryland.

In 1910 it was announced that a branch railway line was to be built from St. John's to Ferryland and eventually on to

Trepassey to serve the communities of the Southern Shore. One proponent of the venture wrote: "Even if the fisheries not be prosecuted with any further increase...now that the district is to be opened up by a railway, it should certainly awaken a keener spirit of enterprise among the people, and tend to develop some of the resources that have so long lain dormant. The railway has transformed the entire condition of life in Newfoundland, and therefore it is only reasonable to claim that the district of Ferryland will derive equal benefits from this same agency."

The purpose of the proposed line was to increase the prosperity of the Shore in all industries of fishing, farming, logging, and even mining. Chiefly, it was thought that a line to Trepassey would make it "a winter port for the island, enabling Steamers to transfer mails, passengers and freight at times when St. John's might be blocked with ice, and possibly in the future becoming a port where big Atlantic Liners could call the whole year round and thus avoid the divergence from the regular route which a call at St. John's would imply."

The line would be about 100 miles long and would run through or within immediate touch of every important settlement along the Shore so that "the people of these thriving fishing and farming settlements will be able to derive the very best advantages from this construction."

Some of the advantages hoped to be gained were the employment its construction would bring to fishermen, farmers, miners, and lumbermen "who would also find opportunities in that section for the employment of their energies." It was also hoped that the Shore's "varied attractions for the tourist and sportsman would be rendered available so that it might become, as its advantages warranted, a summer resort for the people of St. John's and visitors to the colony, all of whom would receive from the warmhearted people of the district a cheery welcome..."

The Ferryland Lighthouse. Built at Ferryland Head on the Downs, it was constructed in 1870 and put into operation the next year. The light tower and dwelling house was designed by a St. John's contractor, William Campbell, and built by a St. John's mason, Thomas Burridge. The tower was a masonry structure sheathed in iron and housed a fixed dioptric light supplied by Stevenson's of Edinburg. The house was a duplex designed to accommodate the lightkeeper, his assistant, and their families. It operated for over 100 years until it was shut down in 1980. (Photo: Courtesy of K. Mooney, *Southern Scenics.*)

The official sod-turning took place on May 9, 1911 attended by Government officials, representatives of the Reid Newfoundland Company, which would build the railway, and attract hundreds of curious onlookers. Construction began immediately and two months later it was reported that "exceptional progress" had already been made.

"The construction of the line," it was reported, "the grading of the road bed having been completed by Coronation Day [May 24] to Witless Bay...the Company entertains the hope of having the whole rail bed constructed right to Trepassey before the snow comes and the rails at least as far as Renews...which section will probably be operated the coming winter. This will make a record unique in local annals and will give the people of the greater part of Ferryland district an opportunity of enjoying the advantages of daily intercourse by train with the capital, which they have been waiting the past thirty years to avail of."

Despite financial hurdles the line was completed and the Southern Shore Branch R.R. was opened in 1914. Probably the most notable run ever made on the Southern Shore Branch Line was the rescue train of February 1918. The special train was hurriedly formed up in St. John's on Sunday morning February 24 to go to the rescue of the SS *Florizel* which had foundered and was breaking up on the rocks of Horn Head just off Cappahayden on the Shore. The "special" was quickly loaded with all the medical and other supplies needed for a winter rescue and packed with volunteer and professional help from doctors and nurses to shipwrights and police officers, and sped to the scene about sixty miles south from St. John's. Bad weather however hampered the rescue efforts, which could not really begin until the rounded up rescue ships arrived some hours after the train. The wreck of the *Florizel* took 94 lives but 44 were saved largely due to the arrival of the rescue train.

The enthusiasm for the development and optimism for the increased prosperity of the Shore did not materialize however. The Southern Shore Branch R.R. enjoyed only a short, languid, unprofitable existence of about fifteen years. It had been hoped that "there is room all along this shore for greater expansion of business and for three times its present population."

The branch line was a losing proposition from the start. The trebling of the population did not occur and neither did the greater expansion of business. Traffic on the line was too light and the loads had to be necessarily lighter because of the light horsepower engines and narrow gauge rails, the slight bridges and steep grades. The biggest factor in its failure was the rates charged for both freight and passengers which were too low to cover the costs of the operation.

On the mainland railway companies could move a ton of freight for the cost of one cent a mile. Along the Southern Shore line the cost to move the same fright was seven and one half cents a mile. By 1931 the Shore Branch of the Newfoundland Railway was closed down permanently and the tracks taken up. Parts of the old track route were later incorporated into the Southern Shore Highway.

The Ferryland Railway Branch Line. Was begun in May 1911 when the sod for the line was turned by the acting premier and other politicians, attended by officials of the Reid Newfoundland Company and hundreds of curious onlookers at the Waterford Bridge Station in the west end of St. John's. (Photo: Courtesy *The Newfoundland Quarterly.*)

By the early 1930s the leading business interest of the Ferryland area was the Tors Cove Trading Company established in 1926 after the Carters of Ferryland had bought up the assets of the Goodridge Company of St. John's. By this time the Labrador fishery was no longer being prosecuted by fishermen from Ferryland and the town's fishery consisted of catches taken more by trap crews and was primarily cod, with some herring, salmon and caplin.

In 1936 Ferryland embarked on the experimental trials of co-ops that were being tested in other areas of Newfoundland. That year one report read: "At Ferryland just before Christmas the Rev, Father Rawlins, an energetic parish priest...organized a Co-Operative Society. By means of a Government loan, the Society purchased the existing fish stores and shop of the Tors Cove Trading Company in Ferryland, together with the stock of goods and book debts of that business, and erected magnificent fish stores, salt store, cooperage, cold storage bait depot and enlarged the public wharf of the place."

The Co-Op showed some success into the 1930s when it continued to provide cold storage and bait freezer facilities for local fishermen. It became known as the Southern Shore Trading Company in the 1940s and in the early 1960s it was bought out by North East Fisheries of Harbour Grace which operated the firm until about 1970.

When the Harbour Grace interests pulled out, a local businessman, Bernard Kavanaugh, converted the fish buying business into a wholesale-retail company, which still serves the many communities of the Southern Shore. By the 1980s the declining fishery all around Newfoundland saw a decrease in the workforce of the industry and many of the Shore's working people sought employment in the service sectors or began commuting to St. John's and other communities for employment.

At the turn of the 21st century, Ferryland survives with a population of about 750, most of whom continue to make their livelihood from a much more diversified fishery which has naturally and necessarily evolved. Since the moratorium on the cod fishery in 1992 the people of the community have turned their hands to any and all species of fish and shellfish which the sea and the seasons will provide.

Ferryland Trains did not bring the prosperity to the Shore that had been envisioned and hoped for. The promise of the railroad as the key to prosperity from the hinterlands did not materialize for the Shore just as it didn't for many other regions of Newfoundland. It took less than eighty years for the entire system to be abandoned island-wide. Tracks were torn up to be shipped to far-off countries like Chile and ties became timbers for community wharves and country cottage patio decks. (Photo: MUN-CNS.)

PROFILE — Bishop James O'Donel: Political Prelate

James Louis O'Donel was Newfoundland's first Catholic Bishop and perhaps the most politic in the island's history. Although he championed the spiritual soul of the Irish community in Newfoundland he also showed a loyalty to the Protestant British Crown that bewildered many by its apparent contradiction.

O'Donel was born in Knocklofty, Tipperary, Ireland in 1737. His father was a well-to-do farmer who sent him and his brother to the Franciscan seminary of St. Isadore in Rome to become priests. O'Donel was ordained in 1770 and for seven years taught theology in Prague. In 1777 he returned to Ireland and was appointed Head Prelate of the Franciscan Order in the County of Waterford.

In 1783 O'Donel was appointed official priest to the Irish Catholics of Newfoundland as the British authorities were fearful there would be unrest if the colonials were left without a pastor. O'Donel was to be a sort of circuit pastor, since permission had not yet been given for the Catholics to build churches or establish parishes in Newfoundland.

He arrived in Newfoundland with high credentials. Pope Pius VI had endorsed him as the first Prefect Apostolic to be assigned to British North America. Upon his arrival in St. John's he began the construction of a chapel and then began his rounds of the outports. In Harbour Grace he decided another chapel should be built then moved on to a visit of the

Southern Shore. There he encountered the rogue priests who were on circuit from Placentia to Bay Bulls. In addition to administering the spiritual needs of the people, a couple of them also preached revolution.

Bishop James Louis O'Donel. First Apostolic Prelate in British North America and first Roman Catholic Bishop of St. John's and Newfoundland. (Photo: *The Benevolent Irish Society of St. John's, Newfoundland: 1806–1906*. 1906. [MUN-CNS].)

O'Donel drew up a set of diocesan statutes and guidelines to be followed by the priests in their service and established parishes at St. John's, Harbour Grace and Ferryland and appointed particular priests to administer to each. Almost immediately he was confronted with problems. The rogue priests, who almost to the man had been in the colony without proper permission since the time of Lord Baltimore and the establishment of his Colony of Avalonia, persisted in instigating the Irish population to outright insurrection. O'Donel ordered them to both desist their rabble-rousing and settle down in the parishes he had created or leave the colony. A couple persisted in their rebellious ways and the Bishop was kept busy travelling his parishes trying to quash any rumblings of rebellion.

He had problems with the other side of the religion coin also. In 1786 Prince William Henry, son of King George III, later to become King William IV, arrived in Newfoundland for a tour of duty with the Royal Navy. He landed in Placentia, one of the hotbeds of the rogue priests and soon found himself in conflict with O'Donel's Papist parish and the legal practice of Catholicism to which he was bitterly opposed. The Prince encouraged his magistrates and Navy and Army officers to openly obstruct and oppose the Catholic Church's influence among the Irish population. William Henry then journeyed to St. John's where he crossed paths with O'Donel himself.

Prince William Henry, later to become King William IV, had a run-in with O'Donel in St. John's. The inebriated Prince not only hurled insults at the clergyman but also a small dagger which fortunately only caused the priest slight injury. (Photo: *Wikipedia.*)

The Prince was playing billiards with some of his cronies in a tavern on the "Lower Path" [Water Street] one day when he looked out the window to see O'Donel strolling down the street. Either out of drunkenness or at the taunting of his companions, the Prince flung open a window and shouted insults at the clergyman and then for good luck, as O'Donel put it, "finally bursting into open madness, with violence hurled an iron file [small dagger] from a window" which struck the priest in the shoulder slightly injuring him.

News of the incident soon spread throughout the town and the Irish Catholics were outraged. There was fear that a full-scale riot would erupt, but O'Donel pleaded for calm and as the governor hastily had the drunken Prince whisked out of town the priest prevailed on his congregation to keep the peace.

O'Donel continued to visit his parishes and at Ferryland found one of the rogue priests, Father Power from Placentia, and the encounter precipitated the riots of the winter of

1788-89. This incident and others he faced during his turbulent tenure showed O'Donel's absolute abhorrence of mob rule. He hated the violence and anarchy that accompanied revolution, such as was being reported from France at the time, and discouraged his parishioners from any violent resistance to the duly constituted authority of the land, even if it was British.

Bishop O'Donel built the first Catholic church in Newfoundland in St. John's in 1786. The church was later named the Chapel of St. Louis, possibly in honour of Bishop O'Donel whose second name was Louis. (Photo: *The Benevolent Irish Society: St. John's, Newfound-land: 1806–1906.* 1906 [MUN-CNS].)

O'Donel's problems with the English administration continued over the next several years. Successive governors were not as tolerant of the improving situation of Catholics as some of the previous ones and constantly reported to England the concerns of the Church of England clergy about the spread of "Popism" in the colony. They claimed that Irish Catholicism was becoming a political force in the colony and the latest Governor, Mark Milbanke, threatened new restrictions on the Irish Catholics. Again O'Donel showed his astuteness as a politician and assured the governor of the loyalty of his flock to the Crown.

O'Donel managed to keep both sides placated until 1791 when a Chief Justice appointed to the colony assured that the Irish Catholics would be free from harassment. By 1796 O'Donel had established a stability among the Catholics and Protestants that prompted the Irish to petition Rome to have him installed as their Bishop. The Pope agreed and on September 21, 1796 Newfoundland was elevated to the status of a Vicariate-Apostolic and O'Donel was consecrated as Bishop of Newfoundland at Quebec City by Bishop Hubert, making him the first English Bishop in British North America and its only one outside the diocese of Quebec.

The Bishop's loyalty to Crown and Country was sorely tried again in 1799 and 1800. When he heard rumours that a planned rebellion by the Irish in Newfoundland would take place in empathy of the Rising of '98 in Ireland, O'Donel went to the governor and warned him of the possibility. Again he was showing his utter disgust and fear of violent rebellion.

As O'Donel himself recorded, Catholicism had to uphold authority, and the French and Irish Rebellions had "brought indelible infamy on our Holy Religion." The Bishop believed that change could be brought about through peaceful means rather than by the bloody tactics of revolutionaries. He even condemned those among his own congregation who advocated violent revolution. After he had helped diffuse the potential situation of revolt he wrote of those who attempted to organize it that he had been "fortunate enough to bring the maddened scum of the people to cool reflection and dispersed the dangerous cloud that was ready to burst on the principal inhabitants."

The aborted revolt of 1800 facilitated O'Donel's work in Newfoundland and he enjoyed a greater cooperation with the British authorities. By 1804 his health had deteriorated and he requested a successor be appointed for him. In 1807 Bishop O'Donel returned to England where he spent a year or so in Bristol before he returned to his home in Waterford.

In April of 1811, the Bishop fell asleep in his reading chair one evening and the candle beside him tipped over and started a fire. Although he was not seriously burned, his failing health and gaining age contributed to the stress which was blamed for his death two weeks later on April 15th.

This Silver Urn valued at 150 guineas was presented to Bishop O'Donel by the grateful populace of St. John's, given "in testimony of his pious, patriotic, and meritorious conduct," upon his departure for Ireland in 1807. (Photo: *The Benevolent Irish Society St. John's, 1806–1906.* 1906.)

Bishop James O'Donel was seen by some of his contemporaries as a vacillating prelate, a puppet of the administration who would not support the reactionary aspirations of some of his congregation. But above all he was a level-headed, masterful politician whose insight and temperate thought allowed the Catholic Church to establish itself and flourish in the volatile and prejudiced years at the turn of the nineteenth century in Newfoundland.

CHAPTER IX

Avalonia Today — Fact and Fiction, Legends and Lies

𝕬**balonia** today has a second, fledgling resource, which is steadily growing and beginning to flourish. Tourism is perhaps the second largest source of livelihood of the community as it begins to reveal the treasures and secrets of its almost 500 year history.

In addition to its natural scenic attractions, Ferryland capsules nearly 500 years of history to entice the curious. Traces of everything from prehistoric aboriginal natives to the first migratory European fishermen, from roving pirates to first attempts at colonization in America, to warfare between rival nations for possession of the North American continent; all have left their tracks and artifacts to reveal piece by piece their unique and intriguing stories. Visitors can investigate its historic treasures at the Ferryland Museum and the Colony of Avalon site where their displays and interpretation centres reveal in great detail the sights, scenes, and spirit of Lord Baltimore's Colony of Avalonia of almost 400 years ago.

Archaeologically, Ferryland is a treasure trove. An archaeological dig begun in the Pool area of the Downs almost twenty years ago continues into the year 2005. During that time archaeologists from Memorial University have unearthed at least six sites in an area of about two hectares in and around the Colony of Avalon in the Pool area. Remains of a Mansion House, a stone waterfront, a forge, gardens, defenses (a fort), and a planter's house and well, have been excavated and identified. The archaeological evidence shows that: "by 1630 the Ferryland waterfront resembled stonebuilt West Country ports more than the wooden fishing rooms seen elsewhere in Newfoundland."

It is not known for certain if the Mansion House is that of Lord Baltimore or of later origin. The chief archaeologist at the site said: "we could say that just maybe we've found the Mansion House, where the Calverts lived back in 1628-29." However, he adds that, "...We'll have to wait for more excavation to be sure just who lived in this house and exactly when it was built in the first place." The dig continues into 2005 on the just over ten acres or so that Baltimore's Colony of Avalon is believed to have occupied.

Excavation sites at the Ferryland dig: 1990s–2004. (Photo: NLHF.)

To highlight the historical heritage of the town, the Colony of Avalon Foundation is diligently at work promoting and preserving the local history of Ferryland. Each year the Foundation plays host to the "Colony of Avalon, once a gateway to North America.... Now a window to the past.... Where visitors can see working archaeologists as they uncover what life was like more than 300 years ago in a 17th century colony..." The Foundation's modern and impressive Interpretation Centre is home to the treasures of the dig.

The Colony of Avalon Foundation Logo. (Photo: COAF.)

Of the thousands of artifacts already found, the Colony of Avalon Foundation has identified and catalogued and pieced back together items for hundreds of displays that are recognizable and definitely identifiable objects, and have gathered probably thousands of bits and pieces of other artifacts. Some have been sent to institutions to be restored and preserved, but many are also on display at the Colony of Avalon Foundation Interpretation Centre in Ferryland.

At the Interpretation Centre visitors can view artifacts from the past 400 years which reflect the history of the area before the coming of the colonizers, and the everyday life of the settlers of the early 17th century: everything from Beothuck Indian stone arrowheads to cannonballs from the days of conflict with the French and Dutch, and everyday items such as padlocks, gold rings, keys, clay pipes, pottery, ceramics and stoneware, glassware and glass beads, iron axe and tool heads, nails and other ironmongery, coins and official seals and medals, and even pieces of gravestones.

Artist's depiction of what the Ferryland Waterfront looked like in Baltimore's time. Late investigations are of the opinion that the waterfront premises there "resembled stone-built West Country ports more than the wooden fishing rooms seen elsewhere in Newfoundland." (Photo: Courtesy of Michelle O'Connell, the Colony Cafe, Ferryland. Painting by Stewart Montgomerie.)

Under the auspices of the Colony of Avalon Foundation, visitors to the site can see the actual dig taking place during the summer months, observe Conservators in the labouratory as they piece the artifacts back together, and visit reconstructed 17th century English Country Gardens which include a kitchen garden, an herb garden, and a country gentleman's garden.

Walking Tours are also available to view the hundreds of displays within the Interpretation Centre, and a site by site account of the excavation grounds with their reconstructed or preserved remains of Lord Baltimore's Colony of Avalon.

The digs over the past years have settled some other interesting questions for historians and archaeologists. The finding of native Beothuck Indian artifacts dispels the long held view of many historians that these natives did not at any time occupy the Avalon Peninsula. The few amateurs who believed otherwise can now feel vindicated by the finds at the Ferryland digs.

The Colony of Avalon Foundation Building. The modern complex houses the artifacts collections and displays from the Ferryland dig as well as modern labs to do
the work of archaeologists and conservators in its extensive Interpretation Centre.
(Photo: Courtesy of K. Mooney. *Southern Scenics.*)

A long held legend or lie from the Ferryland area
concerning the Beothucks tells of a band of the Indians who
showed up in the hills around the Butterpots in the last years
of the 1790s, possibly because they had a trading rendezvous
with Kerrivan's Masterless Men who by then had penetrated
north into Trinity Bay where the Beothucks were known to
have lived in considerable numbers. According to the legend,
the encounter was not a peaceful one as the Indians apparently met with the wrong group and one of them, reportedly
a man named Robert Carter, shot and killed one of the
Beothucks.

If such an incident did occur it is more likely that the
Indian was a Micmac as some of that tribe were still known to
inhabit parts of Placentia Bay long after the French had left
the island. What is curious about the incident is the fact that
the Indian would be identified as a Beothuck since the
settlers of Ferryland were well-acquainted with the Micmac
hunters and trappers of the area by this time.

It is also not known to history or legend if the Robert Carter named, who was described as "a well-to-do planter from the settlement" was a relative of the Carter who heroically left to defend St. John's in 1762 while his wife and the women of Ferryland forted up on Buoys Island to defend their settlement from an attack by the French.

As with the Beothucks, Ferryland has several other stories in its traditional history — legends, which unlike the hard-fact history of documentation are often dismissed as folk tales, but which sometimes have turned out to — like many legends — have a basis in fact if not indeed be totally true. The legend of the Masterless Men is perhaps the most prominent of Ferryland's traditional history stories, but there have been others, a couple of them only recently confirmed by the "hard-facts' school of adherents themselves."

One native-born Ferrylander and long-time recognized and accepted authority on the community's traditional history recently related how they, as a self-proclaimed adherent to the hard-facts school, had one of the long-time legends of the town confirmed to them. For years they had heard the story of Dead Man's Gulch where it was said that about forty fishermen lost their lives at some point in the town's history. Seeking shelter from a savage storm the men sought refuge in the gulch only to have the cliff above them cave down on them.

The person explained their skepticism by saying: "I always found it hard to believe that there could have been such a catastrophe in such a small community and never once hear of it...." But in recent years they read an article in a 1904 magazine and there in its pages was a recounting of the Dead Man's Gulch incident. As the reader commented: "I had to swallow my theory of myth!"

Even 21st century science with its cutting-edge technology and documented evidence is not above being bested by the long-time legends of traditional history. Only about ten years ago the dig at Ferryland was itself responsible for verifying one of Ferryland's oldest legends. For years while the dig was in progress there had been "several versions of a legend about a long-lost well, with a different location for each over an area of several acres." The story went that the legendary well had existed for some long years, but when a child fell into it and drowned it was filled in never to be used again.

Somewhat skeptical, the excavators reluctantly agreed to dig for the well and upon consulting an older gentleman who lived nearby it were directed to dig in a precise spot. Before the day was out the archaeologists had uncovered the remains of a 25 foot deep well that clearly showed that it had been purposely filled in at one time.

Excavations confirmed that the well dated to the late 17th century and that it had been filled in late in the 18th century. "There seemed to be little doubt," investigators reported, "that the well was that of the legend." When asked how he knew of the exact location, the old gentleman who had pointed it out replied: "Because I paid attention." He then went on to explain who told who, and who said what over an almost two hundred year period. As the investigator commented: "The moral of the story is obvious."

In addition to the historical and archaeological interests of the town, there is also the natural splendour of the area to attract the attention of visitors and downhomers alike. Today, tourism is fast becoming Ferryland's second industry. The work was started for them over 200 years ago by a young Royal Navy midshipman whose ship, HMS *Boston*, was sent on station to Newfoundland in 1794. Aaron Thomas's ship put into port at Ferryland on its tour of duty and he spent several days there and recorded in his journal his impressions of and experiences in the settlement.

"About a mile from Capelin Bay," Thomas recorded in his journal, "is Ferryland where there is a considerable settlement. Near two hundred Houses and Hutts constitutes this place. There are some good Stores [fish stores] and much Trade is carry'd on in Fish. There is a Harbour of difficult access; before it lies Ferryland Head and the Isle of Boise."

During his stay at Ferryland, Thomas spent his leisure time exploring and viewing the surrounding country. In his journal he recorded lengthy accounts of his sojourn and the sights around the settlement as well as many of his experiences there.

"On our passage to this Bay the Sea afforded to our sight some very extraordinary phenomenas [sic] of Nature, so plentiful were the Islands of Ice on this Coast at this time that I counted Twenty-nine in view at one time."

Thomas also noted some of the natural scenic landmarks of the area in his strolls around Avalonia. "On the point off Ferryland is a remarkable Rock call'd Hares Ears, so named because its appearance having an affinity to the Ears of that Animal. Between Cape Broyle and Cape Race are these singular, almost mountainous rocks call'd the Butterpots. They are situated on the edge of a Mountain about five miles inland and extend in length, I suppose, three miles. There are a number of these huge Rocks, and their sponsors Christened them Butterpots from their resemblance to the domestic utensil. They are very remarkable Seamarks and are so high that they are seen from Trinity and Conception Bays which are on the Northern Shores."

Today, boat tours around Ferryland Head, the Downs, Buoys Island, and the Shoals and the Pool of Ferryland Harbour afford visitors the chance of seeing icebergs, nesting sea birds and breaching whales up close. Aaron Thomas described the spectacle of breaching whales at Ferryland over 200 years ago.

"I was walking one day on Ferryland Head, looking towards the Sea. I saw a thick vapor or mist rise in a narrow compass out of the Ocean near the shore. I thought it was the smoke which issued from a Gun when fired, only it rose in a larger column...the person who was with me immediately said: 'It is a whale blowing.' This is the first time I ever saw a motion of one of these creatures. Presently we saw the fluke of his tail and the enormous Fins on his back. He kept rolling and Moving about in chase of a fish called Capelin."

In addition to the historical heritage and natural beauty there is the traditional culture of the area that is alive and well. In the past couple of decades efforts to promote the history, heritage and cultural traditions of the Shore have been vigorously pursued by the Town of Ferryland and the Ferryland Development Association who in conjunction with the town's other institutions have fostered a steady increase of interest in the area.

In recent years Ferryland has played host to more than 10,000 visitors per year, most of whom come for the summer festivities and to experience the "Irish Heart of Newfoundland." The popularity of the area and the success it enjoys is due largely to the local institutions and people who work year-round to make their attractions so popular. Chief among these is the Southern Shore Folk Arts Council and its many members who give tirelessly of their time and energy to organize, promote and participate in local projects that keep the spirit of the community alive throughout the year.

Anyone who is familiar with the Southern Shore at all knows that its people, perhaps the people of Ferryland in particular, need little reason to show their hospitality and have a party – or a "time" as it is known locally. The people all along the Shore bill themselves as the Irish Heart of

Newfoundland in the Heart of the Irish Loop and few would dispute this claim.

Southern Shore Folk Arts Council Logo. (Photo: SSFAC.)

The "Shamrock Festival" Logo. (Photo: SSFAC.)

For almost forty years now the town of Ferryland has been celebrating an anniversary which was originally instigated by the Americans of Ferryland's sister colony in Maryland. On September 20th, 1967 the then governor of Maryland, Spiro Agnew, declared that day to be Maryland-Ferryland Day in honour of the Canadian Centennial celebrations being held that year. The gesture was not only in recognition of Canada's Centennial, but also acknowledged the long ties between the colonies of Avalon and Maryland by way of their Proprietorship in the name of the Calvert family.

The Great Seal of the State of Maryland acknowledges this connection by its inscription which translates: "Cecilus, Absolute Lord of Maryland and Avalon." Cecilus was Lord Baltimore's eldest son who took over the running of the Maryland colony as well as the Colony of Avalon when his father died. The Seal also bears two figures: one a farmer grasping a hoe representing the planters of Maryland, and the other holding a fish symbolizing the fishermen of Avalon.

In July of 1983 the Newfoundland Government officially declared Ferryland/Maryland Day would be held annually on the fourth Sunday of July and celebrated with a Seafood Festival. The Festival was held for about ten years when the failing fishery threatened to scuttle it. But into the breach stepped the resourceful Ferrylanders who devised other attractions to celebrate their community day.

They decided they would have an even bigger time and extended the holiday to a two-day affair to be held on the third weekend of July. In the early 1990s organizers launched the very successful and increasingly popular "Southern Shore Shamrock Festival." Held on the Saturday before Ferryland/Maryland Day it is a two day event (some would suggest three days) which is opened by "Lord and Lady Baltimore" apparelled in period costume.

Ferryland Arts Centre Building. This recently refurbished "store" is today home of the Southern Shore Folk Arts Council annual "Dinner Theatre" as well as year-round "special events."

The combined Shamrock Festival and Ferry-land/Maryland Day celebrations see a variety of events and attractions highlighted by performances of Irish-Newfoundland music and local Dinner Theater presentations. "Down-Home" cuisine is in abundance with seafood still the main fare, but many other "Newfie" scoffs are also served up with flavourful flare. Other attractions feature arts and crafts exhibits and sales with local handiworks, replicas of 17th century North Devon pottery, Sgraffitto Bowl, and seventeenth century dolls sold in several Craft Stores and Gift Shops. Amusements are plentiful with games of chance, wheels, and dory races. The highlight of the festival is undoubtedly the almost non-stop music performed by both local and c.f.a. (come from away) groups and solo artists, and the Dinner theater performed by local artists. The event winds up with a gala time with a traditional "scoff and scuff" where all have a good time of food, fun, and fiddling.

The Southern Shore Annual "Shamrock Festival" is fast becoming one of Newfoundland's most popular musical events. (Photos: Courtesy of K. Mooney, *Southern Scenics*.)

Despite the hardships of nearly 400 years, the small settle-ment that was and is Ferryland has survived handily. In the face of several and severe enemies; wars, total and partial destruction over the centuries; in the face of inner turmoil, power struggles, and religious intolerance, its people perse-vered. When the tiny colony's founder deserted his dream-land of an Avalonia in the New World with the comment that he had committed the place "to fishermen who are better able to encounter storms and hard weather," he probably had no idea of just what storms they would encounter or just how hardy a people he had left his legacy to in trust. He would not have been disappointed...

The Ferryland Dinner Theatre is an annual event of the Southern Shore Folk Arts Council that presents summer performances of theatre and other entertainment by local participants.

The Baltimore
Steak House
Hotel | St. John's

The "Baltimore Steakhouse" was a recent popular dining spot in St. John's.

Town of Ferryland Coat of Arms. The Arms is quite reminiscent of the Ferryland-Maryland connection with its shield of the Calvert Family Arms and the Supporters of the original Seal of the Colony of Maryland, the Planter of the Colony of Maryland and the fisherman of the Colony of Avalon. (Photo: Town of Ferryland.)

Ferryland Today: Looking west from the Downs across the Pool and the town to the Gaze beyond. (Photo: Courtesy of K. Mooney, *Southern Scenics.*)

Ferryland Today: Looking east from the Gaze across the Pool and the Downs out to sea and the old world beyond. (Photo: Courtesy of K. Mooney, *Southern Scenics.*)

Today, Lord Baltimore and his dream are not only remembered on the Shore however. All over Newfoundland hotels, motels, restaurants, lounges and other facilities have sported his name from time to time. In St. John's a city street in a quiet northwest end of the city was named for him over fifty years ago — a quiet residential area of retirees with a "prettie little street" and lush "country gardens" — just as Baltimore envisioned almost 400 years ago. Perhaps his far-sighted dream has been realized.

PROFILE — Sea Stories: Rescues, Wrecks, and "Wrackers"

Ferryland, like most communities in Newfoundland and Labrador, has a long seafaring tradition: born, nourished, and grown out of the briny ocean. No doubt many heroic and tragic encounters have occurred when man and nature met without malice. Tragic encounters need no recounting as they are too well remembered by those who suffered from them, but heroic counterparts are all too often forgotten.

Several such incidents occurred in or near Ferryland during its long history. The earliest was probably the wreck of the ship uncovered in the 1990s in the Pool of Ferryland harbour. Details of this ship's encounter with fate are unknown to date, but details of other wrecks and rescues have been well-documented.

One of the most dramatic and Herculean rescues recorded in the sea sagas of Ferryland was the rescue of part of the crew of the brigantine *Heather* on March 25, 1865. The ship was caught in the ice off Cape Spear and was in danger of being crushed on the rocky shoreline. The captain, Richard Ash, allowed most of the crew to abandon the vessel while he and three mates remained aboard. Captain Ash and his mates stayed with the ship until it was crushed on the rocks by the ice then grabbing what they could carry abandoned the ship for the ice floes. Once on the ice pans they found they could not reach shore and drifted out to sea.

They drifted south for two days on their ice floe when they were spotted off the Downs at Ferryland Head. Ten "brawny bravos" of the settlement took to the ice heaving waters in a small boat and picked up Captain Ash's three companions but had to leave him for a second trip. As the boat returned for the captain, a storm that was brewing broke and the men were blown out to sea about forty miles where they spent a miserable night.

The next day they made landfall at Witless Bay about thirty miles northward. From there the rescue boat tried to make St. John's but further bad weather forced them to land in Petty Harbour. From there the men were carried on to St. John's by horse and sled. From there the Ferryland lads looked for a boat home that they wouldn't have to row.

On March 31, 1865, Captain Ash expressed his gratitude to the "bravos" from Ferryland in a St. John's newspaper. "The undersigned, part of the crew of the brigantine *Heather* lost at Cape Spear on the 25th inst., desire to return their most sincere thanks to the boat's crew who so nobly risked their lives to rescue them from the ice, and in so doing were exposed for nearly thirty hours in an open boat in this inclement season."

The rescue boat's crew were named by Captain Ash as: Francis Geary, John Costello, William Morry, Marmaduke Clowe, Henry Morry, Richard Sullivan, Thomas Morris, James Sweeney, Peter Kelly, and John O'Keefe. Ash reported that "these last two were frostbitten." A mild understatement one would think to describe men who had spent two days in an open boat in winter weather and constantly rowing to cover a distance of more than fifty miles.

In 1913 the ship *Evelyn*, a brigantine, or schooner, captained by Edgar Burke and crewed by six men, was en route to St. John's from the West Indies when it was caught in a raging winter blizzard on January 10th. The ship was just off Ferryland Head when the storm hit and tried to make it into the harbour. It was dashed on the shoals just north of Buoys Island in its attempt and the crew scrambled ashore onto the rocks below the craggy cliffs on the south side of the island. On shore a group of men noticed the sinking ship through a break in the driving snow. Seven men launched a skiff and rowed out to the island through the raging sea and blinding snow and succeeded in landing on the island on the opposite side from the wreck.

The Ferryland Lighthouse Today: The Lighthouse today lies in "ruins," mute testament to the many ships it saved from the stormy seas around Ferryland harbour. (Photo: B.F.)

After scaling the icy cliffs, they crossed to the north side and the stranded crew below, but because of the strong wind could not get a rope down to them. The smallest man of the lot, Will Furlong, was then lowered down the steep side of the cliff with a rescue rope and one by one the captain and his men were hauled up the ice covered cliffs.

The rescued and the rescuers now had to get back to shore which proved to be another dangerous ordeal as their skiff had suffered damage in landing and was taking on water. Frantic rowing and bailing kept the leaky boat afloat and all hands made it ashore where the wrecked crew were sheltered for the night and carried on to St. John's the next day by horse and sled.

The seven "boys" of Bouys were named as three Barnable brothers: Jim, Bill and Jack; Howard Morry; and two Deveraux brothers, Mike and John. The wiry rope climber Furlong, was a brother-in-law of the Barnable boys.

The story of the wreck of the SS *Florizel* on February 23-24, 1918 is well-documented in Newfoundland history. When the ship went aground on the rocks off Horn Head near Cappahayden in a savage winter storm on the night of February 23, the men of Ferryland were some of the first on the scene to lend a hand as rescuers. All attempts that night however, by the Ferryland men and others from nearby communities to launch rescue boats into the heaving seas had to be abandoned, the crews of the boats themselves barely escaping with their lives.

The SS *Florizel* foundering on the rocks of Horn Head at Cappahayden in February of 1918. (Photo: *Newfoundland Quarterly.*)

By morning's light the seas had subsided a little and a few brave rescuers managed to reach the stricken ship and bring in a few of the survivors. The main effort had to await the arrival of four rescue ships on their way from St. John's whose progress to the scene was greatly slowed by choking ice all the way down the shore.

The rescue took more than 27 hours from the time of the first distress signal until the last soul was rescued, so severe were the weather conditions and dangerous and difficult the rescue. Of the 138 people aboard the *Florizel* only 44 were saved. Thirty-five Medals of Bravery were awarded in the days following the rescue, some of them won by the men of Ferryland.

The ship SS *Torhamvan* was en route to either Trois Rivieres or Montreal on the afternoon of October 29, 1926 when she went ashore on the shoals of Ferryland harbour and was completely wrecked. The steamship was one of a new line owned by mercantile interests in TORonto, HAMilton, and VANcouver, thus the unusual name. It usually operated between Montreal and Vancouver but that day was on a trip from St. John's to Quebec. It became lost in a dense fog off the point on the north shore of Ferryland Harbour and had been sounding its horn in distress for some time as it tried to maneouver between Goose Island and the "point." People had gathered on the shore in response to the *Torhamvan's* horn, but could not see the ship through the dense fog and the ship could not see their signals.

About five o'clock in the afternoon came the unmistakable sound of metal grinding on rocks which told the onlookers that the vessel was aground. A group of Ferryland men quickly pushed their boats into the water and headed for the crushing sounds through the treacherous "gap." In the high seas they managed to rescue all of the crew of the stricken ship who said that none of them had any idea they were so close to shore.

The crew was cared for a day or so at Ferryland then shunted off to St. John's. The people of Ferryland wondered why the ship had not seen the light from the lighthouse on the Downs and all agreed that the fog must have been one of the thickest ever seen on the Shore.

Many tales are told about the wreck of the *Torhamvan* and its subsequent salvage. The Salvage Commission was soon on the scene, but not before the "wrackers" had finished their work. They helped themselves to whatever cargo they could tote away — everything from paint to jam, to lard, soap, macaroni, and any other number and variety of goods. Some years later a group of youngsters admitted to having run off with boxes of soap powder that bore the brand name "Gold Dust," believing the boxes contained the real thing.

The town of Ferryland also benefited from the salvage. It claimed, and still possesses some say, two bronze statues which for years stood sentinel to the doors of Holy Trinity Church, as well as a large crucifix which adorned the interior of the church for some years. The *Torhamvan* was gradually eroded by the washing seas until today only the rusting boilers remain as a testament to a wreck in one of the thickest fogs to be seen in Ferryland harbour in over seventy-five years.

SOME SAGE SAYINGS FROM THE SHORE

The Southern Shore bills itself as the "Irish Heart of Newfoundland" and one has no difficulty finding that heart alive and well all along the Shore, perhaps especially so in Ferryland. It is particularly evident in the almost innate and intrinsic humour, sometimes melodramatic or even mildly profound, but often tempered with a wry and sometimes outright funny sense of comedy. There's no problem catching a perplexing pearl of wisdom or a downright ribald rib of humour as one gets ready at the kitchen table for a game of 120s, or "railroad," and a sit-down to a "savage mug-up" or to enjoy "a jar." These are a few of the tidbits of wit and wisdom one might hear from the sages along the Shore.

The older the fiddler...the sweeter the tune...

Don't mistake an old goat's beard for a fine stallion's tail...

Drink is the curse of the land...
    It makes you fight with your neighbour...
        It makes you shoot at your landlord...
            ...and it makes you miss him!

There never was an old slipper but there was an old sock to match it...

Firelight will not let you read fine stories...
But it's warm and you won't see the dust on the floor...

As the old cock crows...the young cock learns...

It's for her own good that the cat purrs...

Even a tin knocker will shine on a dirty door...

An old broom knows the dirty corners best...

'Tis no use to carry an umbrella if your shoes are leaking...

A silent mouth is sweet to hear...

He'd offer you an egg if you promised not to break the shell...

There never was a shabby sheep that didn't like to have a comrade...

To a raven...even her own chick is white...

Any man can lose his hat in a fairy wind...

No matter how often a pitcher goes to water it is always broken in the end...

A wink is as good as a nod to a blind horse...

There'll be white blackbirds before an unwilling woman ties the knot...

Men are like bagpipes...no sound comes from them until they are full...

Every patient is a doctor after he's cured...

Never give cherries to a pig...or advice to a fool...

You'll never plough a field by turning it over in your mind...

The oldest pipe gives the sweetest smoke...

Marriages are all happy.... It's having breakfast in the morning that causes all the trouble...

A scholar's ink lasts longer than a martyr's blood...

Take gifts with a sigh...most men give to be paid...

What butter and whiskey will not cure...there's no cure for...

The Irish forgive their great men when they are safely buried...

The best way to keep loyalty in a man's heart is to keep money in his purse...

A wild goose never raised a tame gosling...

The longest road out is the shortest road home...

A narrow neck keeps the bottle from being emptied in one swig...

And...
> Here's to a long life and a merry one
> A quick death and an easy one
> A pretty girl and an honest one
> A cold beer and another one...

May you live to be one hundred years, with one year extra to repent!

BIBLIOGRAPHY

Agriesti, D. Series of Articles for the *Ferryland Historical Society*. 1970s–1990s. "Ferryland: Lord Baltimore's Colony

"Lord Baltimore's Ferryland."

"Items of Interest on Ferryland's History."

"Ferryland Facts."

"Ferryland Fortifications."

"A Tour Through Ferryland's Past."

"Some Women in Ferryland's Past."

Barakat, Robert A. "Some Comments on Lord Baltimore's House at Ferryland." *Newfoundland Quarterly*. Vol. 8 No. 3. St. John's, NL. 1976.

Brown, Cassie. *A Winter's Tale: The Wreck of the Florizel*. Doubleday Canada Ltd. Toronto, ON. 1976.

Browne, W. J. "Some Notes For A History of Agriculture." *Newfoundland Quarterly*. Vols. 42–47. St. John's, NL. 1942–1947.

Davis, Kelly. "In John Guy's Footsteps." *The Evening Telegram*. St. John's, NL. Oct. 1, 1994

Dawe, David. "Peter Kerrivan and His Masterless Men." *The Newfoundland Herald*. St. John's, NL. June 20, 1998.

Drodge, Eldon. *Kerrivan*. Jesperson Publishing. St. John's, NL. 2001.

Dyer, Allison. "Historical Roots." *The Evening Telegram*. St. John's, NL. October 2, 1999.

English, L. E. F. "Sir David Kirke." *Newfoundland Quarterly*. Vol. 53 No. 3. Fall, 1950.

————- *The Story of Placentia.* Star of the Sea Association. Placentia, NL. 1962.

Fardy, B. D. *Under Two Flags.* Creative Publishers. St. John's, NL. 1987.

Flanagan, Susan. "The Other Guy." *The Evening Telegram.* St. John's, NL. July 6, 1996.

Foster, James W. and Beta Manakee. *The Lords Baltimore.* Enoch Pratt Free Library. Baltimore, Maryland. 1934.

Gullage, Peter. "Farillon." *The Express.* St. John's, NL. January 6, 1991.

Harper, J. R. "In Quest of Baltimore's House at Ferryland." ms. *Presentation Convent Archives.* St. John's, NL. n.d.

Harrington, Michael. "Brave Rescue by Ferryland Men." *The Evening Telegram.* St. John's, NL. March 31, 1989.

——————— ---- "Falkland and the Youngsters." *The Evening Telegram.* St. John's, NL. Oct. 2, 1978.

——————— ---- "The Ferryland–Maryland Connection." *The Evening Telegram.* St. John's, NL. July 22, 1985.

Hiller, J. K. *The Newfoundland Railway : 1881–1949.* Newfoundland Historical Society. Harry Cuff Pubs. St. John's, NL. 1981.

Hohn, E. "D'Iberville In The North." *Newfoundland Quarterly.* Vol. 69 No. 2. Fall, 1972.

Horwood, Harold. "The Masterless Men of the Butterpots." *Newfoundland Quarterly.* Vol. 65 No. 2. St. John's, NL. 1966.

Howley, M. F. "Mason's Map and Vaughan's Vagaries." *Newfoundland Quarterly.* Vol. XI No. 2. Summer, 1911.

Humphreys, John. *Placentia: The Military History of Placentia.* National Museums of Canada. Ottawa. 1970.

Johnston, Wayne. *Baltimore's Mansion.* Vintage Canada. Toronto. 2000.

Lahey, Raymond J. *James Louis O'Donel In Newfoundland.* Newfoundland Historical Society. Harry Cuff Pubs. Ltd. St. John's, NL 1984.

LeMessurier, H. W. "An Ancient Reminiscence of Cape Broyle." *Newfoundland Quarterly.* Vol. 13. No. 4. St. John's, NL. 1913.

Mannion, John. J. Ed. *The Peopling of Newfoundland.* Memorial University Press. St. John's, NL. 1977.

MacAfee, Michelle. "Artifacts By The Millions Found In Ferryland." *The Evening Telegram.* St. John's, NL. July 28, 1998.

McCarthy, M. C. *The Irish In Newfoundland 1623–1800.* Harry Cuff Pubs. St. John's, NL. 1983.

Moore, Smith G. "Robert Hayman and the Plantation of Newfoundland." *Newfoundland Quarterly.* Vol. 60. No. 2. St. John's, NL. 1966.

Morris, I. C. "The Southern Shore." *Newfoundland Quarterly.* Vol. 9 No. 4. St. John's, NL. 1910.

Murray, Jane. *The Kings and Queens of England.* Scribner's Sons. New York. 1974.

Murray, Jean. Ed. *The Newfoundland Journal of Aaron Thomas.* Longmans Canada. Don Mills. ON. 1968.

Murray, Miles P. "Forgotten Ferryland." *Newfoundland Quarterly.* Vol. 49. No. 2. St. John's, NL. 1949.

N.A. "The Beginnings of Irish Immigration." *The Rounder.* St. John's, NL. 1982.

N.A. *The Colony of Avalon.* Web Site. (Various Articles) Ferryland, NL. (1990–2005)

N.A. "D'Iberville's Trail." *The Shoreline.* C.B.S. NL. 1996.

N.A. "Digging Up The Past." *The Evening Telegram.* St. John's, NL. July 28, 1998.

N.A. "The Ferryland Railway." *Newfoundland Quarterly.* Vol. 11. No. 2. St. John's, NL. 1911.

N.A. "The Kirke Connection." *Decks Awash.* M.U.N. Press. St. John's, NL. 1976.

N.A. "Kirke of Ferryland." *The Wayfarer.* St. John's, NL. n.d.

N.A. "Naval Battles and Buried Treasure." *The Rounder.* St. John's, NL. 1982.

N.A. *Newfoundland and Labrador Heritage.* Web Site. (Various Articles) Memorial University of Newfoundland and Labrador. (CNS). St. John's, NL. (1990–2005)

N.A. "Sir David Kirke's 17th Century Mansion Brought to Light." *The Evening Telegram.* St. John's, NL. August 16, 2001.

N.A. "The Southern Shore." *The Rounder.* St. John's, NL. 1982.

Neary, Peter and Patrick O'Flaherty. Eds. *By Great Waters: A Newfoundland and Labrador Anthology.* University of Toronto Press. Toronto, ON. 1974.

——————— *Part of the Main: An Illustrated History of Newfoundland and Labrador.* Breakwater Books. St. John's, NL. 1983.

O'Neill, Paul. "Lord Baltimore and the Avalon Plantation." Newfoundland Historical Society. ms. St. John's, NL. 1977.

Piercy, Heide. "Finding Footprints." *The Evening Telegram.* St. John's, NL. July 30, 1994.

Pope, Peter E. "Documents Relating to Ferryland: 1597–1726." (35 Docs. Cited.) *The Colony of Avalon Foundation.* Ferryland, NL. 1993.

Proulx, Jean Pierre. *Placentia: Newfoundland.* Parks Canada. Government of Canada. Ottawa, ON. 1979.

Prowse, D.W. *A History of Newfoundland.* McMillan and Co. Ltd. London and New York. 1895.

Pumphrey, Marilyn. "Genealogical Society Discovers Criminal Connection." *The Express*. St. John's, NL. July 29, 1992.

Rowe, Frederick W. *A History of Newfoundland and Labrador*. McGraw-Hill, Ryerson. Toronto, ON. 1980.

Smallwood, Joseph. Ed. *The Book of Newfoundland. Vols. I-VI*. Newfoundland Book Publishers (1967 Ltd.). St. John's, NL.

Smallwood, J. R. and C. F. Poole, R. H. Cuff, R. D.W. Pitt. Eds. *The Encyclopedia of Newfoundland and Labrador. Vols. I-V*. Newfoundland Book Publishers (1967 Ltd.) and the J. R. Smallwood Heritage Foundation. St. John's, NL. 1981–1994.

Sparkes, Paul. "A Modern Look at Ferryland." *Newfoundland Quarterly*. Vol. 68 No. 2. St. John's, NL. 1968.

White, Jack A. "The Streets of St. John's: Baltimore-The Name Is Steeped In History." *The Evening Telegram*. St. John's, NL. July 19, 1990.

BERNARD D. FARDY was born in St. John's, Newfoundland in 1949. On completion of high school he left the province and travelled and lived for several years in western Canada and the United States. He returned to Newfoundland in 1971 and studied Forestry Technology at the Cabot Institute of Applied Arts and Technology. Upon graduation he was employed by the Newfoundland Government and worked for twenty-five years with the Department of Forestry and Agriculture as a Forestry, Land Use and Cartographic Technician. An avid student of Canadian and Newfoundland history, he has written several books including: *Jerry Potts: Paladin of the Plains*; *Capt. David Buchan in Newfoundland*; *William Epps Cormack: Newfoundland Pioneer*; *Under Two Flags*; *Demasduit: Native Newfoundlander*; *Liefsburdir: The Vikings in Newfoundland*; *John Cabot: The Discovery of Newfoundland*; and *Before Beaumont Hamel: The Royal Newfoundland Regiment 1775–1815*. His articles have also appeared in the *Newfoundland Quarterly* and *Canadian Frontier*.